FUNDAMENTALS OF SINGING

FUNDAMENTALS OF SINGING
FOR VOICE CLASSES

CHARLES EDWARD LINDSLEY
California State Polytechnic University, Pomona

Wadsworth Publishing Company
Belmont, California
A Division of Wadsworth, Inc.

Music Editor: Sheryl Fullerton
Production Editor: Deborah O. McDaniel
Design: Andrew H. Ogus
Copy Editor: Zipporah W. Collins
Illustrators: Dick Cole and Jane McCreary
Signing Representative: Lorrenda Phillips

Printed in the United States of America

2 3 4 5 6 7 8 9 10—89 88 87 86 85

ISBN 0-534-04608-8

Library of Congress Cataloging in Publication Data

Lindsley, Charles E.
 Fundamentals of singing for voice classes.

 "Song anthology": p.
 Bibliography: p.
 Includes index.
 1. Singing—Methods. 2. Songs with piano. I. Title.
MT825.L64 1985   784.9'3   84-19485
ISBN 0-534-04608-8

DEDICATION

For Carol Vaness, Mary Heyler Mundy, Melanie Chambers Alpert,
Debra Rye, Lisa Johnson, Timothy Bullara, James Anthony Brown,
William New, Michael Gomez, Daniel Terzo, and many others of my
successful former students whose vocal training began in a voice class.
To such highly motivated students, past, present, and future, I
dedicate this book and enthusiastically devote my teaching energies.

Contents

CONTENTS

Song Anthology Contents

POPULAR AND MUSICAL THEATER SONGS

OPERA ARIAS

DUETS

PATRIOTIC SONGS

List of Illustrations

PREFACE

You cannot learn to sing from a book. While a well-written book may inform you and guide your learning by organizing materials so that you approach the basic concepts of tone production in a systematic manner, you still need a teacher to monitor your efforts. Only a skilled teacher with a keen ear can determine if you are on the path to a correct singing technique—that is, a technique that enables you to sing beautifully and effortlessly for a lifetime. No book can replace a good teacher's ability to *listen* analytically to your singing efforts and respond appropriately. However, particularly in voice classes, both the teacher and the student can be greatly aided by a carefully organized textbook.

The purpose of this text is primarily to organize teaching materials. It is designed to help both you and your teacher make the voice class an effective learning experience. The book provides

(1) basic information about the voice and how it behaves, clarified by detailed illustrations, (2) exercises for developing a solid vocal technique, with many vocalises for improving skills, (3) a body of vocal literature drawn from an unusually wide range of musical styles, to offer beginning song materials for students with widely divergent singing aspirations, and (4) a structured and systematic presentation of these elements, planned and organized to accommodate a one-semester or one-quarter college or university beginning voice course.

A major premise of this book is that singing is a learned behavior requiring the development of certain coordination skills. I believe that singing is not an activity limited to a gifted or talented few but rather an activity accessible to all physically normal, motivated, and reasonably disciplined persons. Further, I believe that the level of skill and singing excellence that students achieve will vary with their individual physical attributes, their desire to sing well, and the quality of both their guidance and their practice. Such premises have not always been accepted, and there are certainly those who subscribe to the notion that only a chosen few possess the "God-given talent" to become singers.

Surely part of the mystique surrounding the art of singing arises because much of vocal behavior remains little understood, even late in the twentieth century. Since a large part of the control required in singing lies below the level of consciousness, direct approaches to teaching singing technique have not always been forthcoming. Over two hundred years ago Johann Mattheson (1681–1764), a renowned German singer and teacher of singing, admonished his students:

> Go to a lonely place out in the fields, dig a small but deep hole in the earth, place your mouth over it and scream the voice into it as high and as long as may be without too violent an effort. Through this and similar exercises the tools of sound, in particular of boys whose voices are breaking, will become exceedingly smooth and clear like a wind instrument which, the more it is used and cleansed by the air the more delightful it will sound.[1]

Through the centuries literally thousands of "methods" of singing instruction have emerged (many, fortunately, having a greater scientific basis than the one just described), each claiming to be correct. In reality, there are as many methods as there are teachers, because teachers of singing, like singers, are unique. Each has somewhat different ways of achieving desired results. However, among the myriad of current methods there seem to be two broad, general approaches, at least in this country: the *psychological image* approach and the *mechanistic* approach. Both have certain strengths. The psychological image approach makes use of already learned, nonsinging concepts and behaviors as a means of achieving vocal skills ("imagine you are biting an apple, in order to bring the *ah* vowel more forward," or perhaps, even more indirectly, "imagine your voice flowing freely, like a running stream"). The mechanistic approach endeavors to impart an intellectual understanding of the physical behavior entailed, whether or not it is consciously controllable. Exclusive use of either approach has disadvantages: the psychological image approach gives singers little or no understanding of the physiology and behavior of the voice, limiting

---

1. Quoted in Frederick Husler and Yvonne Rodd-Marling, *Singing: The Physical Nature of the Vocal Organ* (London: Faber and Faber, 1965), pp. 84–85.

their ability to build it or care for it properly, while the mechanistic approach alone may produce singers who possess only singing *technique*, with little or no ability to sing musically.

This textbook endeavors to integrate the two approaches. It subscribes to no single method of voice culture. I have gathered material from many sources, both the books and articles listed in the Bibliography and firsthand experience in working with numerous outstanding voice teachers. The organization of the text is based on the most effective of the teaching procedures I have developed during fifteen years of successful voice class instruction. I make no apology for including some rather detailed anatomical and physiological materials (if your teacher finds certain portions too technically complex for his or her purposes, they may be easily omitted); they can enhance your understanding of both the behavior of the vocal mechanism and the basic concepts of singing well. In my own classes I have observed that students are usually curious about their vocal anatomy and physiology. They want to understand what is happening when they sing. They are not satisfied simply to accept some vague imagery or to imitate a teacher's examples. In short, they want to *know* how their voices behave and why. I feel strongly that students should have the opportunity to understand these concepts in detail, and that this will help them to become more intelligent singers and will teach them how to build, maintain, and protect their voices for a lifetime.

The songs at the back of this book were chosen with the needs of diverse beginning voice students in mind. Whatever your singing aspirations for the future and your present background, you should find at least some songs that appeal to you and are within your artistic grasp. As your singing skills develop, your interest in new and unfamiliar song literature will probably increase. If your singing background has been primarily in popular songs, you may develop an interest in art song literature, for instance. This collection contains songs from musical theater, arias from opera, folk songs, art songs, and popular songs, selected to accommodate divergent needs and tastes. The songs have also been chosen with varying vocal range requirements in mind and exhibit different levels of musical difficulty, from simple settings of folk songs for true beginners to operatic arias for students with at least some prior training. Some of the song texts (particularly in the musical theater and operatic selections) were written for specific voice-types. For example, one piece may be specifically intended for soprano, another for baritone, and so forth. If you are unsure whether a given song is well suited to your voice in its present stage of development, consult your instructor before you begin preparing it for performance.

I urge you, as a beginning singer, to take advantage of every opportunity for vocal development that this book and your voice class afford. Read the book carefully, attend the class regularly, and practice faithfully. The voice you wish to develop is the only one you will ever have. It is precious and worth your every effort. Keep this in mind as you work to improve your singing skills.

ACKNOWLEDGMENTS

Bringing a book such as this to print requires the skills of many other persons than its author. I wish to acknowledge my appreciation, first of all, to the talented people on the staff of Wadsworth Publishing Company who so ably assisted me in this project. Particularly, I would like to thank Sheryl Fullerton, music editor, who saw promise in my proposal and had faith in my abilities to complete the manuscript and to secure permission to use the music I had selected. I am grateful to Zipporah Collins, my copy editor, whose language skills greatly improved the clarity and accuracy of my manuscript. I wish to express special appreciation to Debbie McDaniel, my production editor, whose abundant talents were displayed again and again in the final stages of putting the book together. I wish also to acknowledge the helpful comments and suggestions of my reviewers: LeGrande Anderson, Fresno City College; Dianne Davidson, Los Angeles Valley College; John L. Dietz, Indiana University of Pennsylvania; Jane Hardester, El Camino Community College; and June D. Swartwout, West Virginia University.

The initial preparation of my manuscript would not have been possible without a sabbatical leave granted by California State Polytechnic University, Pomona, Hugh O. LaBounty, president. I wish also to thank my colleagues on the faculty and staff of the music department of this campus for their personal support. Their interest in my project was a continual source of encouragement.

Finally, I would like to thank my students, who were my inspiration to write the book in the first place. It is their desire for knowledge, their appreciation for what I am able to teach them, and their motivation to do something worthwhile with that knowledge that provides my most valued sense of purpose.

1
PREPARATION

THE VOICE CLASS: GETTING THE MOST FROM IT

Can a voice class really teach you to sing? The classroom is the generally accepted arena for studying history, mathematics, biology, and even fine arts such as art, dance, and drama. But voice? Traditionally, serious voice training is undertaken in private studios, as the study of other musical instruments is. The one-to-one teacher-student relationship is generally considered the most effective means of training singers. Undeniably, every voice student is unique. Each voice possesses particular strengths and weaknesses. How can a variety of individual vocal attributes be dealt with successfully in a common experience?

Despite their differences, voices are voices, and proper management of them for singing requires students to acquire certain common skills. Just as any group of people bring varying degrees of individual knowledge and skill to a class in other disciplines, so a group of would-be singers bring varying levels of vocal expertise to a beginning voice class. Disparities in previous experience will certainly be evident in the first few class sessions, but they in no way reduce a student's potential to develop personal vocal skills. The pace at which each student does this will ultimately have little to do with the pace of the class as a whole.

The teaching approach in a beginning voice class is actually much the same as that in other disciplines: The group meets together on a regular basis and an instructor disseminates information, along with examples, exercises, and demonstrations. Each student is then expected to spend an equal, if not greater, amount of time in individual study and practice outside of class. Periodic *recitations* (performances of songs) by each individual take place at appropriate intervals in class, so that the student's progress can be noted and so that class members have a valuable opportunity to learn *from each other*—perhaps more directly than in classes in most other disciplines. A final assessment of each student's vocal development is made in the form of an exam—usually a singing performance that is expected to reflect all the skills and artistry the student has gained as a result of the class.

It is true that at *advanced* stages of vocal training it is virtually impossible to deal with the very specific characteristics of individual voices in a group rather than individually. But at early stages of vocal study a great deal can be accomplished through group training. In fact, the voice class has some distinct advantages over individual studio training, and these can enhance and even accelerate early learning experiences.

Participants in a voice class usually get to know each other very well. You may be surprised at how early in this course you will know everyone else's name. This is partly because there is constant communication among class members due to the nature of the class, and partly because of the expressive and directly personal nature of singing itself. This familiarity is a significant benefit of the class approach, for the social atmosphere that emerges is almost always a supportive one. The prevailing attitude of "we're all in this together" is an important source of encouragement to everyone in the group. This comfortable social situation promotes very valuable positive-reinforcement activity. When this happens, there is an unmistakable atmosphere of "we want you to succeed" that fosters courage in even the most timid of students.

Another advantage of group study is the frequent opportunity it offers each student to sing before an audience. To be able to perform once or twice a week for informal critical review is a benefit not enjoyed by most voice students studying privately. It provides both performing experience for each student and excellent opportunities to learn by example. You will observe others grappling with some of the same problems you are experiencing. This is a valuable didactic process that may well clarify in your mind exactly what your difficulty is and may stimulate possible solutions. Also, watching others begin to demonstrate conspicuous vocal development can assure you that the methods and techniques "work," and this will fortify your own efforts. Sometimes a healthy spirit of competition emerges among certain members of the group, again encouraging more diligent effort than if each student were working individually. Perhaps an even stronger motivating force is offered by the occasional student whose performance is truly outstanding. The power of inspiration is substantial.

The class approach to vocal study is not new. It has been used successfully both in this country and abroad for many decades. It is further validated by the fact that many singers (both "classical" and "popular") with highly successful careers had their first voice-training experiences in a high school or college voice class. Whatever your goals as a singer may be, if you are a student with little or no prior voice training and you have decided to begin voice study in a class, you have probably made an excellent choice.

CAN ANYONE BECOME A SINGER?

"Singing is not a God-given talent bestowed upon a limited favored few. It is possible for all who possess a voice with which to speak, to learn to sing."[1] The ability to sing beautifully, contrary to a popular notion, is not a *gift*. It is a learned behavior. It is, however, a behavior that requires the possession of extraordinary skill in use of the vocal mechanism. This skill is present in no one at birth; it must be developed. It is quite unlikely that an infant (even a gifted one) isolated from society before he or she had learned to produce controlled singing tones would ever learn to sing in the *bel canto* manner.[2] It is just as unlikely that such a child would ever learn to run the four-minute mile. Both these activities, along with countless others, require highly specialized training and guidance. Just as running the four-minute mile requires that runners learn to move their legs with unusual speed and coordination and to control other body functions (such as breathing) in an extraordinary way, so does the highest quality of singing require singers to learn to use their voices and control other body functions (again, such as breathing) in an extraordinary way. It is virtually impossible for such skills to be developed without the assistance or example of others who either have already mastered them or understand them intimately.

   Also, contrary to popular opinion, great singers are not born with great voices. Humans, on the whole, are equipped with surprisingly similar vocal equipment. Just as the ears, eyes, and noses of physically normal persons have similar functional capabilities, so do their voices seem to have similar capabilities—except, of course, that the physical size and shape of the organs and the sex of the individual directly determine pitch range, tone quality, and to some extent, volume. As Van Christy, a noted singing teacher and author of numerous books on singing, stated, "The facts appear to be that all normal human beings possess an adequate vocal instrument only awaiting liberation and knowledge of how to use it for beauty of production." He elaborates: "Generally speaking, the physical structure of the average voice is sufficiently suitable to allow for beautiful, artistic singing, provided there is sufficient native talent and musical sensitivity combined with persistent study and practice under wise guidance."[3]

   If all this is true, why is there such a difference between the sound of your voice and that of the vocal "star" you admire so much? The real variance in vocal talent—

---

1. George Oscar Bowen and Kenneth C. Mook, *Song and Speech* (Lexington, Mass.: Ginn and Co., 1952), p. vi.
2. The term *bel canto* is translated as *beautiful singing* but is generally used to describe the Italian vocal technique of the eighteenth century, which placed great emphasis upon the *beauty* of the vocal sound.
3. Van A. Christy, *Expressive Singing*, 3d ed., 2 vols. (Dubuque, Iowa: Wm. C. Brown Co., 1967), 1:2.

and it is a wide one indeed—is in the *skill* with which different individuals use their voices. Just as certain individuals seem to be "naturally" better coordinated in athletic activities than others, certain singers are better coordinated vocally, or develop vocal coordination more quickly. Thus, the answer to our question, "Can anyone become a singer?" is an emphatic "yes!"—given normal circumstances. Can anyone become an *outstanding* singer? The answer to this is another matter. No one, not even the finest voice teacher, can determine immediately a given individual's vocal potential. Many superb singing voices have developed from voices that at first seemed to show little promise. If you are an average college or university student enrolling in a beginning voice class, you have every reason to expect considerable vocal development. A physically sound and healthy person who has not already learned to sing incorrectly (with resulting faulty habits already ingrained) should expect rapid progress. There are a number of factors that can hasten and enhance your vocal development.

HOW TO PREPARE FOR VOICE TRAINING

Learning to sing is not so much a matter of training the *voice* as it is training the ears, the breathing mechanism, the resonators, and even certain extraneous muscles. The quality of these body functions will largely determine the rate and degree of vocal development. Of course, as in all other physical arts, the ultimate skill is mental control.

Training your mind for singing is largely a process over which you alone have control. It cannot be done for you. Although you may be guided, informed, and inspired by your teacher, by professional performers, and by your peers, little actual change will take place without your own initiative. You will, no doubt, need to be taught what is involved in correct singing technique; you may need to be shown examples of good and poor vocal production; you will certainly need to be taught what you must do to build your own correct technique. (Many concepts are not universal—what works for one singer won't necessarily work as well for another.) You will need the assistance of an alert, knowledgeable, sensitive teacher with an extraordinarily keen ear, plus examples of professionals you admire and feedback and support from your classmates and the friends for whom you sing. But beyond this it is pretty much up to you. Little vocal development will take place unless you really *want* and are willing to work for the singing skills you seek. Thus, *self-motivation* will become one of your most important tools for progress.

It is already evident that you want to sing; otherwise you would not have enrolled in a voice class. Your reasons for this desire may or may not be entirely clear to you. Obviously singing has a significant appeal to you. You derive pleasure either from listening to others do it or from doing it yourself—or both. You have, no doubt, discovered that it is enjoyable on many levels: physically, artistically, creatively, and expressively. Pleasure and enjoyment are important motivating forces for any singer and should continue to play an important role in *why* you sing, for as long as you continue to do so. But there are still other satisfactions to be found in this enjoyable and pleasurable activity. One of the most significant, and ultimately one of the most motivating, is the healthy sense of satisfaction that we derive from developing any physical skill—learning to swim, ski, speak in public, drive a car, play the piano, and so forth. We take pleasure in our physical accomplishments, and so we should. They render us more interesting, more intelligent, more confident, more expressive, more complete human beings. In singing, like these other activities, our pleasure in the activity is enhanced as we gain skill in it. This is a great built-in motivator. The greater your singing skills become, the more you will enjoy singing. The more you enjoy it, the harder you will work to become better.

Even before you begin actual vocal study, you can do a great deal on your own to hasten your vocal development by taking steps to strengthen and increase your self-motivation. One of the most direct ways to go about this is to develop an enthusiastic interest in *all kinds* of singing. This may be done by listening to as many vocal performances as you can, on radio, television, and recordings, and by attending as many live performances as you can afford. Begin to develop an analytical eye and ear for these experiences. Don't cease to enjoy them for their own sake but begin to observe very carefully as many aspects of the performances as you can. Also notice your own responses: What appeals to you? What does not? Ask yourself why.

As you examine a wider range of singing activity, bring your own vocal attributes into the picture. Have you ever recorded your singing voice? If not, make a recording of yourself singing a favorite song with appropriate accompaniment. Don't be surprised if you don't sound anything like you thought you would. Most people are incredulous at hearing their own singing voice "from the outside" for the first time. Your first reaction will probably be, "Is that me?" Remember that singers (and speakers) hear themselves largely through bone conduction; listeners hear a singer through air conduction. When you first hear through air conduction what you have always heard before through bone conduction, you are likely to be surprised; but you will know what you *really* sound like. You may like what you hear, and you may not. In any case, after you have become somewhat acclimated to how you sound to other people, begin to analyze the sound of your voice and compare it to performers you have heard recently, both professional and amateur. What is good about your voice? What would you like to change?

The activity described above should be repeated frequently throughout the course. You will find your insights and analyses becoming increasingly accurate. Your knowledge and skill as a singer will also become increasingly sophisticated. You will probably even enjoy the sound of your own voice more and more.

As you expand your awareness of singing and singers, don't hesitate to experiment. For example, try producing a tone on a given vowel sound (*ah*, perhaps) several different ways. First make the tone overly "bright," or blatant, in quality (sing through an exaggerated smile); then produce the same tone with a very "dark" quality (sing through an exaggerated yawn). Then experiment with tone qualities between these extremes. Notice the difference in the sensations you feel and in the ease or difficulty with which you produce the sound. Ask yourself which qualities sound and *feel* best to you. You will discover that *feelings*, that is physical sensations, are your most reliable guide toward beautiful tone production. Explore as many parameters of your voice as you can, through experimentation.[4] Even endeavoring to imitate trained voices similar in range and quality to your own can be beneficial and can often lead

---

4. Be careful not to go to unhealthy extremes, however. Do not do anything with your voice that causes discomfort or pain. Good vocal production is never painful, either to the singer or to the listener.

to new discoveries. Some old-fashioned purists in the voice-teaching profession scoff at this idea, forecasting contrived sounds and possible vocal injury; perhaps they have forgotten how they first learned to speak: by imitation. Imitation is at least a part of the learning process in developing *most* skills. There is no reason to exclude singing. A sensible teacher and a sensible student are not likely to allow either contrivance or injury. Just as the beginning skier is not likely to tackle the advanced slopes the first day out (even though skilled skiers make it look easy), the beginning voice student is not likely to try to imitate Beverly Sills or Luciano Pavarotti on a *fortissimo* high C.

As you begin to discover and develop your singing voice, remember (and take pride in the fact) that it is utterly unique—like all the other components of you as a person. It may have qualities that resemble other voices, but it will always produce a sound that is yours alone. It will reflect your physical makeup, your intellect, and your emotions. These will all be projected through whatever vocal and musical skills you are able to develop. The level of artistry you ultimately reach is largely up to you.

PRACTICE: HOW MUCH, WHEN, AND WHERE

Even a widely experienced teacher of singing cannot predict with accuracy how long it will take a given student to achieve certain artistic goals. A myriad of variables pertain: age, the state of the voice at the beginning of training (whether prior vocal activity has induced faulty habits), the speed with which the student learns (and perhaps *unlearns*), physical condition, degree of motivation, practice habits, and the goal itself. If you are of college age, have a voice that now functions with relative freedom, learn quickly, are in good physical condition, are highly motivated, practice regularly and thoroughly, and have a modest artistic goal, you may be well on your way toward reaching it by the time you finish this course. However, it is not likely that all the variables will be this favorable. If your vocal ambition extends beyond singing for your own enjoyment and that of your friends, and you find you do have a vocal problem or two, upon completion of this course you may wish to pursue private study, and you may need to continue for an extended time.

Vocal practice for the singer is in many ways similar to physical training for the athlete. For successful results in either case, the activity must be regular and thorough. It must be regular because the muscles of the body develop most quickly when subjected to regular exercise; it must be thorough because singing, like other athletic endeavors, involves a large variety of muscles and organs. It is only logical that the amount of time spent in vocal practice each day is not nearly as important as how the time is spent. Fifteen minutes of alert, productive practice will accomplish much more vocal progress than an hour of misdirected work. For the beginning singer, thirty minutes a day, on the average, will probably be sufficient to cover the requisite physical activity of training the voice. However, the amount of time needed may vary considerably, depending on specific problems. Try not to limit yourself to a specific number of minutes. You can progress only as fast as your physical and mental state will allow. If on some days you need a bit more time, give yourself that time.

It is important to begin each practice period in a physically and mentally calm, relaxed state. If possible, actually lie down and totally relax for three to five minutes before you begin to practice. Clear your mind of all extraneous thoughts and your body of all tension. Consciously relax. This simple technique works wonders for an efficient and productive practice session.

Where and when you practice are also important. If possible, practice in a large room with "live" acoustics. A small, dead room will tend to inhibit you and will not allow you to hear yourself as others hear you, since most of the sound is absorbed and little of it is reflected back to your ears. Your practice room should be as soundproof as possible so that outside sounds will not disturb you and you will not worry about disturbing others. Many beginning singers are severely inhibited by the feeling that others may be listening to their singing practice (and possibly passing judgment on its quality).

It is almost essential that the room in which you practice have a keyboard instrument, preferably a piano. Although you should never fall into a habit of "leaning" on the piano while vocalizing,[5] it is helpful for providing a constant pitch reference and for outlining vocalises (singing exercises). It is also important that the piano be kept in tune so that you learn exercises in their exact pitch.

Another important requirement of your practice room is a good, large mirror, preferably full-length. This will allow you a full view of your entire body as you sing, helping you establish habits of good singing posture and correct body alignment. It will alert you immediately to distracting mannerisms and unnecessary facial contortions that may adversely affect your performance.

You will find that your voice functions somewhat differently at different times of the day. Upon arising in the morning, you will probably find that your voice sounds lower than usual. In fact, if you check pitches, you may find that you can sing one to three half-steps lower in the early morning than in the afternoon or evening. The reason for this is that the vocal cords and related intrinsic muscles of the larynx are in their most relaxed, elongated state after sleep, and they may retain more body fluids than usual. Thus they can vibrate more slowly, producing lower pitches. Like other muscles of the body they must be "warmed up" before they are able to contract sufficiently to produce your highest tones. Later in the day you will probably find that the higher tones come much more easily, even if you haven't consciously warmed up your voice. When all of the above factors are taken into account, it becomes apparent that you will obtain the best results if you arrange your practice at the same time, as nearly as possible, each day. You will then become well acquainted with the way your voice behaves, and you will not be confused by changes in its behavior that result merely from the time of day.

Finally, organize your practice routine to group together the activities for accomplishing particular goals. This will fall easily into a pattern after you have been studying voice long enough to be pursuing a number of different vocal skills.

PRELIMINARY SONG PREPARATION

As a new voice student, you need to begin preparing to perform songs in public (for the time being, in class) as early as possible. Even though you will have mastered

---

5. Avoid particularly the habit of practicing while seated at the piano. This could cause a habit of poor posture and may result in a poor breathing technique. Also, the piano can soon become a "crutch," weakening your ability to practice independently of it.

few of the technical skills you seek until well into the course (indeed some will require constant work long after the course is concluded), the "learn by doing" approach is generally accepted by successful teachers as the most efficient. You will find the use of songs far more interesting and stimulating than a steady diet of vocalises and other exercises. Also, songs clearly expose the very weaknesses in technical skills that need to be strengthened, reinforcing your desire to work hard to gain mastery of your voice. Further, there is probably no reward or sense of fulfillment greater for a singer than successful performance of a song before an appreciative audience. The response you receive when you have communicated with your listeners on a musical and emotional level will boost your sense of accomplishment and motivation more than complete mastery of the most complex technical exercise. Of course the likelihood of a successful presentation in this early stage of your vocal development will be greater if you initially choose uncomplicated song material. For this reason the first suggested songs from the collection in this text are the least complex ones. If your instructor suggests or agrees to other choices, fine. Just be sure that the material is reasonably within your technical grasp. Perhaps the most important point to remember in selecting your material is that the songs should appeal to *you* and have meaning for *you* if you are to make them meaningful to your listeners.

If you have had some prior musical training (a prerequisite for a beginning voice course at many colleges and universities), such as piano lessons, study of a band or orchestral instrument, or perhaps a music fundamentals class, song preparation will be much easier for you than for those who have not. The ability to read rhythmic values and pitch intervals is essential if you are to become a skilled singer. It is possible to complete this course without music-reading ability, but learning songs will take much longer and you will require assistance from either your instructor or class members who can read music. If you now lack such skills, you are strongly advised to take a music fundamentals class as soon as possible.

Certainly the least constructive way to learn a song is "by ear"—that is by having someone sing or play it for you until you can repeat it yourself from memory. It is indeed possible to learn songs in this manner, but each time you wish to learn a new one you must go through the same tedious procedure, requiring the time and energy of another person, or at least use of a recording. Far better that you should learn to read for yourself. You will soon become adept at it and will be able to learn several new songs in the time it used to take to learn one.

The following procedure is suggested as an efficient and *constructive* method for learning songs. Not only is it reasonably fast, practical, and effective, but it also assists you in improving your music-reading skills. Follow it carefully each time you begin a new song; the results will reward you well.

1.   First, carefully read the words of the song. (This alone should be an important consideration in choosing or rejecting the song.) Make certain you fully understand the meaning of the text. If the music is of high quality, the composer has obviously considered very carefully every aspect of the poet's words in setting them to music. If you are to convey the ideas of both the poet and the composer accurately, you must have an intimate understanding of what the song expresses.

2.   Next, read through the *rhythm* of the melodic line. If you lack music-reading skills, you will need help. It is essential that you learn to count all common meters and to read rhythmic durations accurately. Don't proceed

beyond this point until you are able to execute the rhythm of the melody correctly from beginning to end. You may either clap or tap the durations or sing them on a single syllable, such as *la*.

3.   Now speak the words *in the rhythmic durations* of the melody. Be sure to hold all long note values for their full value, sustaining only the vowels of the words, never the consonants. Observe all rests accurately.

4.   The next step requires the ability to read intervals of pitch. If you have not yet learned to read pitches, again you will need help. (Do learn to do it for yourself, even though it will probably be very slow at first.) It is best to approach the pitch portion of song-learning at a piano in order to check yourself easily on difficult intervals. *Don't* simply play the melody or have someone play it for you! This is the "easy way out," and your learning process will go no further than that attained by a parrot. Learn to *read* the intervals. At first a good deal of trial and error will be involved, but in time you can become quite skilled. When reading through the pitches the first time or two, ignore the rhythmic values. You have already mastered them separately. It will be easy enough to incorporate them with the pitches once you master the pitches.

5.   After you are sure of the pitches of the melody, sing the melody in the correct rhythm, but without the words. Repeat a nonsense syllable such as *la*. This allows you to concentrate on the purely musical aspects of the song without having to deal at once with all the problems of vowels, consonants, textual phrasing, and so forth.

6.   When you are sure that all the musical aspects of the melody are correct, add the words. Sing the song in its entirety a few times. If particular passages cause difficulties, extract those portions and work them out separately. Don't try the song with accompaniment until you are sure every aspect of your singing line is correct.

7.   Now add the accompaniment. You may be in for a surprise or two if you have not heard the song before. The harmony may not be exactly what you had anticipated in certain passages, and the accompaniment may do unexpected things in passages where you have rests, or in the introduction before you sing. Sing the song with the accompaniment enough times to feel comfortable with it and confident enough of your part so that the accompaniment does not distract you.

8.   Now polish, memorize, and learn to express the emotions, mood, or message of the song. These steps involve a multitude of concerns; mastery of all of them makes an "artist." As a beginner, if you prepare your song carefully, if it is musically accurate, if you phrase the text correctly (breathe in the right places) so the meaning of the words is clear, and if you sing it with conviction and sincerity, you are certain to have a successful performance. Before trying the song out on a live audience, it is usually very instructive to try it before a full-length mirror and a tape recorder. You can then get a reasonable idea of what your audience will see and hear. Don't be too hard on yourself the first few times; remember that you will probably judge yourself much more harshly than your audience will. But do take advantage of the chance to see and hear yourself. Correct the flaws you observe and rejoice in your strong qualities.

9.   It is finally time to sing your song for an audience. Your first performance may be just for a few friends before you sing for the class. Ask for criticism. When you sing for the class the first time, don't be intimidated.

Some of your classmates may sing better than you, and some will undoubtedly sing less well. Remember that you are all learning together, and everyone really is "on your side." Do your very best to *communicate* with your classmates. You have prepared this song carefully, you have strong feelings about it, you are an "expert" on it; now convey all this to your listeners, so that they can share your feelings. Once you are before your audience try not to concern yourself with technical matters. Solve those during classroom exercise sessions and your own practice sessions. Now you are *performing*. Use all of the skills and knowledge that you have acquired thus far, but sing from your feelings and emotions.

10.   Finally, learn from the experience and learn from your audience. Once you have performed, seek the critical opinions of your classmates and your instructor. Ask *yourself* what good feelings you had during the performance and what seemed uncomfortable or unsuccessful. It's a good idea to write all these ideas down. Then remember them when you prepare your next song. However successful or unsuccessful your first performance was, if you apply what the experience taught you, you may be sure the next one will be better.

SINGING FOR AN AUDIENCE: SELF-CONFIDENCE OR STAGE FRIGHT?

The subject of performance in public will be treated in greater detail in Chapter 8, but, since you will undoubtedly be singing for the class before you reach that chapter, some preliminary suggestions are necessary here. It is important that your first performance experiences be successful and rewarding, and fraught with a minimum of anxiety. Then the positive reinforcement you receive will be a powerful motivator for continued diligent work. If, on the other hand, your early performing experiences are negative, the discouragement can be substantial and may make you even more apprehensive about your next effort.

Probably every singer who has performed in public has experienced some self-consciousness. It is a natural reaction to being "in the spotlight." For many people this self-conscious state is not alarming; in fact, the temporary nervousness seems to render them even more alert and energetic than usual. In a performance, this nervous energy puts them at their very best. For others, performing in public causes an intense self-consciousness that is perhaps more accurately called *anxiety*. It can escalate until the body is reduced to unresponsive rigidity. It is difficult indeed to sing well when the mouth is dry, the voice feels tight and thin, breathing is restricted, the legs tremble, the memory seems to have evaporated, and the sweat glands are working overtime. These, of course, are the classic symptoms of *stage fright*—the singer's brand of self-conscious anxiety.

How can you learn to react to performance with good, healthy nervous energy instead of negative, defeating anxiety? You can learn to recognize your physical reactions and use them to strengthen, rather than weaken, your performance. Stage fright is one manifestation of the emotion *fear*. Fear is a natural reaction to what we perceive as *danger*, and public performance can certainly be viewed as a "dangerous" situation, especially to someone who has had limited experience in it.

A first step in trying to overcome fear of singing in public is to analyze the elements of the public performance that you fear, and deal with one item at a time. Do you fear failure? Embarrassment? Criticism? Do you actually fear your audience? (Without it, none of these fears would arise.) Think for a minute. Is your audience hostile? Do its members want you to fail? Do they want to criticize and embarrass you? Your audience is, in fact, a group of friendly classmates, not an "enemy." They want you to succeed just as much as each of them wishes to do well. *They are on your side.* If you think through the worst possible consequences of your singing in public, you can readily put most of your fears into perspective. Even if everything goes wrong—if you make a dozen mistakes, if your arms and legs begin to shake, if your mind goes blank and you have to stop, if your voice just quits on you, if you trip going to or from your chair—will it really be the end of the world? All humans are fallible. The course of human history will not be changed if your performance isn't perfect. The members of this audience that is causing your stage fright will eventually be in the spotlight themselves, and very likely their performances will not be flawless either. You will soon learn to support and reassure each other and, in so doing, see one of the voice class's most valuable advantages in action.

Recognizing the origin of your self-consciousness is a large step toward reducing it from destructive panic to a manageable level of emotional excitement. You will probably always feel apprehension and be somewhat nervous before a performance, even if you become a professional singer. But you must learn to recognize this reaction for what it is: a natural physical response to potential stress or danger. The extra energy and excitement you feel as a result of increased glandular activity in your body can be exploited in a positive way. If you channel this energy successfully, the quality of your work may be *best* under the pressure of public performance. Here are a few suggestions to ensure that success:

1. *Be prepared.* Don't attempt performance unless you *know* your material. Being sure you are adequately prepared, both musically and vocally, will give you an invaluable sense of confidence. Inadequate preparation will destroy that confidence.

2. *Be assertive.* The stage is yours—take it. Assume an air of *wanting* to sing for your audience. (If you didn't want to sing you'd have no reason to be taking this class, would you?) Demonstrate a confidently aggressive approach to performance. Your audience will enjoy your singing more, and so will you.

3. *Concentrate.* Focus all your attention on expressing yourself musically and emotionally. Don't allow extraneous thoughts to enter your mind while you are performing. Don't let yourself become distracted. Think of only this song—these words, this music, and how you can convey them best, coupled with your own feelings, to the audience.

4. *Communicate.* Be an actor. *Live* the ideas of the words and the music. By the intensity of your delivery, *demand* a response from the audience. Expect a reaction, and you probably will get one.

If you put these suggestions into action, your stage fright probably will be long forgotten in the process, and you will put your nervous energy to a very productive and rewarding use. Self-confidence, not self-consciousness, is your goal. You may not be able to eliminate self-consciousness entirely, but that is normal, and the nervous energy it creates can be a constructive force to help you do your very best.

CLASSROOM EXERCISES

One of the most valuable aspects of studying voice in a class is that everyone has a chance to learn from other students as well as from the instructor. It is important that all members of the class get acquainted and get an idea of each other's "talent" (or background of experience) as soon as possible, so that improvements can be observed as they take place. To find out where everyone already *is* vocally, each person must be heard at the first class session. Initially, the class should sing together a song that everyone already knows, perhaps "America" (page 260). This will "break the ice" psychologically, warm up the voices, and refresh everyone's memory of the song. Then each member of the class should introduce himself or herself and tell a bit about any prior singing experience, immediate goals, reasons for taking the class, and other pertinent personal information. Following this introduction, each member should sing one verse of the song for the rest of the class. This will help the other class members to remember each student and establish in their minds the level of her or his talent at the beginning of the course.

While listening to the other singers, consider the following:

1. How do you respond to the singer's vocal quality? Is it pleasant to your ear? Is it too "bright" (shrill, thin, pinched)? Too "dark" (throaty, dull, "covered," unclear)? Is the tone large or small?

2. How well are the extremes of pitch executed? Are the high notes pinched; do they sound tense? Are the low notes "forced", or are they almost inaudible?

3. Is the singer at ease or obviously nervous? (Nearly every class member will probably display some nervousness this first time in front of the group, but in some it will be so intense that it clearly impairs singing ability.)

4. How well does the singer handle breathing? Does he or she seem to run out of breath frequently, or does breathing seem not to be a problem?

5. Notice each singer's stage appearance. Observe particularly facial expressions, posture, and physical gestures. Does the singer seem to enjoy singing?

The instructor may choose to discuss all the performances, or perhaps only one or two exemplary ones. He or she may point out a few traits shared by most members of the class. The most important value of the exercise, however, is to give the class a chance to observe each member's singing ability, great or small, before actual vocal study is begun.

ASSIGNMENTS

1. Read Chapter 2 carefully, giving special attention to the muscular experiments and breathing exercises suggested. Because of their complexity and the need for explanation from the instructor, you will probably wish to wait until the class meets to do the classroom exercises.

2. Select one of the following songs (or another suggested or approved by your instructor) to begin preparing.
   a. "Drink to Me Only with Thine Eyes," pages 168–171.
   b. "My Lady Greensleeves," pages 178–183.
   c. "Scarborough Fair," pages 194–196.

Actual performance may not take place for several class sessions. The instructor may present the songs to the class either by singing them or by leading the class in reading through them together.

3. Try to take in a live vocal performance this week. Be prepared to describe it briefly to the class.

2
RESPIRATION

**BREATH: THE FUEL
FOR SINGING**

Without proper functioning of the fuel supply system, no mechanical engine will operate effectively. If you have ever tried to drive an automobile with a faulty fuel pump, you will understand the point. No matter how perfect the condition of all else about the car, it will not run properly if the fuel pump is defective. Trying to sing without correct breathing technique is analogous; if breathing technique is incorrect, nothing else in the singing process will function ideally. It is not by accident, then, that the subject of breathing for singing comes at the beginning of our study of vocal production.

Breath, or rather the air column supplied by the breath, is quite literally the energy source that sets the vocal cords (or vocal *folds*, to be described later) into vibration. Conscious control over this energy source on the part of the singer will in large part determine the energy available to the vocal apparatus for producing singing tone. Before learning how much conscious control is possible and how to apply it, it is essential for you to understand some basic mechanics of the human breathing system. A close examination of Figures 2.1 and 2.2 will help to clarify a description of the physical activity involved.

THE PHYSIOLOGY OF BREATHING

When you breathe deeply you will notice expansion and contraction of the *chest*. If you examine closely what else happens, you will notice expansion and contraction of the *rib cage* too, all the way around to the back. You will probably see even more pronounced activity in the *abdominal region*. There are many different respiratory processes taking place at the same time. These are usually placed in three basic categories: *clavicular*, or chest (sometimes called "shoulder") breathing; *diaphragmatic*, or abdominal, breathing; and *costal*, or rib, breathing. Clavicular breathing is not of much interest to the singer because it offers no control over exhalation and therefore is inefficient for the production of tone. It also easily results in shallow breaths and poor posture, and it can cause muscular tension in the shoulders and neck. The most efficient breathing technique for singing is a combination of the latter two types, abdominal and rib breathing. It is usually called *diaphragmatic-costal* breathing. While the coordinated muscular activity in this technique of breathing is

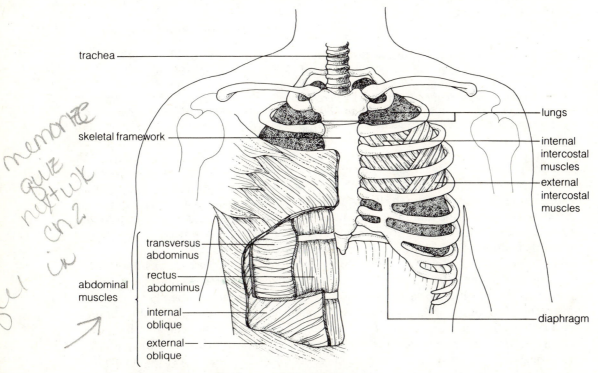

Figure 2.1   The human breathing system
The act of singing requires training the entire breathing mechanism to behave in a consciously coordinated way.

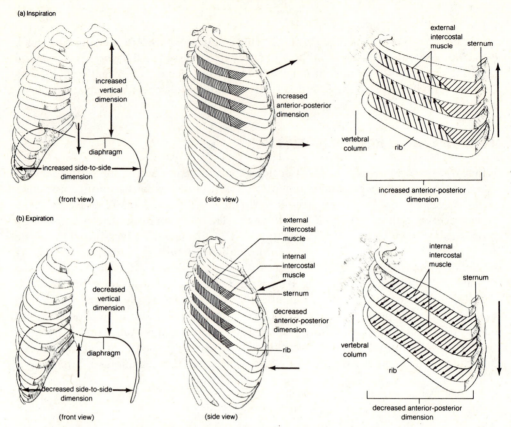

Figure 2.2   Interaction of the diaphragm and the intercostal muscles
During inspiration (a) the diaphragm and the external *intercostal muscles contract. In expiration, (b) and in phonating, or producing vocal sound, those muscles relax, while the* internal *intercostal muscles and certain of the abdominal muscles contract. (From Joan G. Creager,* Human Anatomy and Physiology *[Belmont, Calif.: Wadsworth, 1983], p. 545.)*

exceedingly complex, what the singer *feels* is very simple: conscious expansion-inhalation, contraction-exhalation. Both the thoracic (chest) and the abdominal cavities expand, drawing air into the lungs. When these cavities contract, the air is forced back out. However, the kind of conscious control over this process that is required for well coordinated and highly efficient breathing for singing generally demands more than simply thinking "expand, contract; expand, contract."

 In order to control your breathing process for singing purposes, it is important to note that the muscles involved are for the most part *voluntary/involuntary*. Like the muscles controlling the eyelids, they can either function automatically as needed to sustain life or be engaged by conscious command. Your breathing process functions naturally when you are asleep, but you can also consciously hold your breath if you choose. In learning to breathe correctly for singing, you have to discover the parameters of control that you have over certain of these muscles. The easiest way to begin is to observe the actions of each of the important ones separately.

The important rib muscles are called the *intercostals* (so named because they run between the ribs). There are two sets, the *externals* and the *internals*. When you inhale, the external intercostal muscles contract, pulling the ribs outward and upward. The internal intercostals pull in the opposite direction, inward and downward, assisting in exhalation. To feel this activity effectively, place your hands across your lower ribs with the fingers nearly touching in front. See Figure 2.3(a). As you inhale watch the movement increase the distance between your opposing fingers; as you exhale they will come close together again. Concentrate on voluntary control of this rib movement. Now bend over at a right angle and place your hands in a similar fashion on your back, observing the same activity on the portion of your ribs close to your backbone. See Figure 2.3(b). Again concentrate on moving the muscles voluntarily. To prove that you have conscious control over these muscles and that the movement of the ribs is not caused merely by normal lung expansion, hold your nostrils with your fingers, keep your mouth closed, and move the ribs in and out. Feel this activity with the other hand.

(a)   (b)

Figure 2.3   Demonstration of intercostal activity in breathing for singing
As inhalation occurs, expansion and contraction of the rib cage is produced by the intercostal muscles, not only in front (a), but also at the sides and in back (b). This is readily observable by placing the hands on the ribs in these areas and breathing normally.

You may have heard singers or teachers of singing use the phrase "sing from the *diaphragm*" or "support with the *diaphragm*." While the intent was undoubtedly good, this phraseology is virtually meaningless. While the diaphragm is the largest, the most powerful, and certainly one of the most important breathing muscles, its function is really limited to one process—inhalation—and one cannot *sing* while inhaling.

The diaphragm is a large, double-dome-shaped muscle that lies midway between the thoracic cavity and the abdominal cavity. Look back at Figure 2.1. It creates an airtight wall between the thoracic organs (lungs and heart) and the abdominal organs (stomach, kidneys, liver, and so forth). Like all other muscles, the diaphragm can contract, or pull, in only one direction. When the diaphragm contracts, it moves down, significantly enlarging the size of the thoracic cavity. This creates a partial vacuum, reducing the air pressure in the lungs, which in turn causes outside air to rush in to equalize the pressure. When the diaphragm relaxes, it moves back up to its original position, increasing the air pressure in the lungs and causing them to expel most of the air previously drawn in. Although singers can train the diaphragm (a voluntary/involuntary muscle like the intercostals) to descend voluntarily and to remain in a contracted position for an extended period, they can do little to improve its ability to *release*. Thus, exerting conscious control over the exhalation process requires the engagement of yet another group of muscles.

There are actually four primary pairs of muscles that control *exhalation:* rectus abdominis, obliquus externus abdominis, obliquus internus abdominis, and transversus abdominis. For the sake of simplicity we will consider these all together under the term *abdominal muscles*. See Figure 2.1 earlier. When these muscles contract, they press against the abdominal cavity, which ultimately exerts pressure on the diaphragm. This pressure can greatly assist speedy expiration of air from the lungs by strengthening and hastening the return of the diaphragm to its relaxed, uncontracted state.

To become better acquainted with the sensations of abdominal breathing, lie flat on your back, elevating your head slightly with a book or a small pillow. Place your left hand on your chest and your right hand on your abdomen. See Figure 2.4. Breathe naturally and somewhat deeply, as if asleep. You will notice substantial movement under your right hand, but only slight expansion and contraction under your left. For the most part, this is the way correct breathing for singing feels. Concentrate on these feelings. Exaggerate the movements. Hold the expansion in the abdominal area. Try pushing the air out quickly by contracting the abdominal muscles suddenly. Inhale again. Now release the air very slowly and evenly. Begin to learn what it feels like to control these muscles. Now stand up and interlace the fingers of both hands together in front of you. See Figure 2.5. Place your hands in this cupped position just below the navel. Pull your hands in toward you and slightly up while exhaling. Feel the sensation of actually pushing the air out. Now relax your hands and at the same time consciously relax your abdominal muscles. Literally let your belly drop. Notice how this action draws air into your lungs. Pull your hands in toward yourself again, this time tensing your abdominal muscles. Feel the strong exhalation. Then, as you inhale, relax these muscles and drop your hands. Repeat this exercise for a time, remembering all the sensations you feel. Now remove your hands from the activity entirely. Experience the sensations of the abdominal muscles and the diaphragm doing all the work. It is especially significant to condition the abdominal muscles to relax sufficiently when you inhale. If they remain tense, the diaphragm cannot move

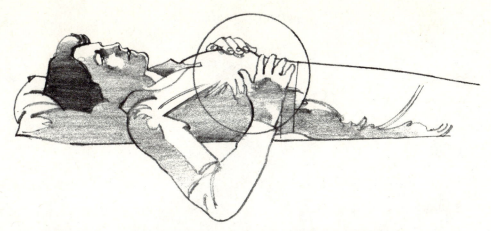

Figure 2.4   Discovering diaphragmatic-costal breathing

Manual examination of normal muscular activity in involuntary breathing (as in sleeping) will reveal the same kind of behavior as is required for the most efficient breathing for singing. Notice that the observable movement, indicating muscular activity, is most pronounced in the abdominal area—the location of the diaphragm and the abdominal muscles—not in the chest area, where the lungs are located.

downward far enough to draw in a full breath. This condition is probably the most common breathing problem among inexperienced singers. The nervousness that usually accompanies public performance often produces some tension in the body; frequently the abdominal muscles are particularly affected. A vicious cycle is then established, as the tension results in inadequate breath, while inadequate breath causes more tension. You can do a great deal to avoid the problem by learning at the outset of your training how to relax your abdominal muscles sufficiently to allow a full-capacity breath.

Perhaps the most significant point to remember about the breathing process is that all the muscular actions work together in one complex, harmonious, cooperative effort. It is somewhat analogous to the highly complicated, shared endeavors of the muscles of the legs and feet that flow into a simple, graceful walk. And, just as the legs and feet can be taught to dance, run, and jump, the breathing muscles can be taught to behave in the special ways required for the production of singing tone.

BREATH SUPPORT AND BREATH CONTROL

You probably haven't heard singers or singing teachers talk about developing better *diadochokinesis* in order to sing better; you probably *have* heard them refer to *support* or *breath support*. If you asked them what support meant, more than likely the answer was somewhat vague. Breath support is a form of diadochokinesis: "the alternate contraction and relaxation of the opposing muscles in muscular antagonism."[1] *Muscular antagonism* refers to the opposition of muscles or muscle groups necessary to accomplish most physical actions. Muscles do not work singly; they work in opposing pairs or groups. In the breathing process, the internal and the external intercostals

---

1.   William Vennard, *Singing: The Mechanism and the Technique*, rev. ed. (New York: Carl Fischer, 1967), p. 260.

Figure 2.5   Manual manipulation of the breathing mechanism

Pressing inward and upward with the hands in the lower abdominal area while exhaling, then releasing while inhaling, will help the student learn the sensations of correct breathing technique for singing. The sense of abdominal muscle contraction for exhalation and relaxation for inhalation must be cultivated until it becomes unconscious.

oppose each other; the diaphragm is opposed by the abdominal group. This opposition of muscles and muscle groups, when coordinated, provides the condition that allows singers to control their breath and tone. They can learn to sing with a very small amount of air or a great deal, producing a soft tone or a loud one; they can hold, or sustain, a tone; they can execute sharp attacks and releases of the tone, or gentle, smooth ones; they can gradually swell the tone from soft to loud, or diminish it. These are but the most obvious results of skilled breath control. Ultimately the sophisticated command singers gain over their breath mechanism allows them greater control over other aspects of tone production as well (such as *resonance*, discussed in Chapter 4). The result is the full range of human expression of which the voice is capable.

A simple exercise (although difficult for certain students at first) to gain coordination of the breath support system is called *pulsation*. It is a repeated application of energy from the abdominal muscles against the diaphragm, producing a pulsing tone that sounds somewhat like a very slow, very wide *vibrato* (vibrato is discussed in detail in Chapter 7). To get an idea of how it works, use one of your hands as an outside, easily coordinated substitute for the abdominal muscles. Place your finger-tips against your abdomen about midway between the sternum (breastbone) and the navel. While singing a sustained tone (*ah* is fine), repeatedly press your fingers gently into the abdominal area and release them in a rapid succession. See Figure 2.6. The resultant tone will emerge as *ah-ah-ah-ah-ah-ah-ah*, with *no complete stoppage of the tone until the breath is exhausted*. Try this several times until you are accustomed to the sensations. Now try to achieve the same result without the use of your hands, using your abdominal muscles in a pulsing manner. (Some students find that an aural image is helpful, such as the sound of trying to start a stubborn automobile engine on a cold morning: *uh-uh-uh-uh-uh-uh*.) If you cannot achieve the coordination to execute this exercise without the use of your hands on the first few tries, don't give up; sometimes it takes quite a while. When you are able to do the exercise with control—able to speed up and slow down the pulsations and to adjust the volume—you are well on your way to achieving the coordination in your breathing mechanism that you need for good breath support and breath control.

Another device helpful for developing coordination in the support muscles is the *staccato* technique. It differs from pulsation in that it uses a complete stoppage of tone between vocalized vowel sounds, and the attack is aspirated: *ha/ha/ha/ha/ha/*

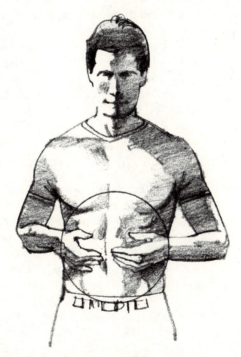

Figure 2.6   Manual pulsation exercise
By alternately pressing and releasing rapidly in the upper abdominal area while sustaining a singing tone (or hum), students can experience the action of the abdominal muscles on the diaphragm. In this exercise the hands, which are highly coordinated, substitute for the abdominal muscles, which are less coor-dinated in early training, allowing the student to experience free, effortless tone production, unrestricted by muscular interference. In order to do this exercise successfully, the body, particularly the abdominal muscles, must be relaxed.

ha/ha. Although executing repeated staccato attacks intrinsically requires even greater muscular coordination (involving laryngeal muscles as well as breathing muscles) than the pulsation technique, it is actually easier to accomplish for most beginning singers than pulsation. The reason is that it is almost identical to a coordination learned very early in childhood and almost by instinct—that involved in laughing. And, of course, most individuals have had a great deal of practice in it over the years. However, learning to exert conscious control over the staccato may requre a bit of concentration at first. A good way to practice this technique and to differentiate it clearly from the pulsation technique in your "sensations memory" is to alternate successions of staccatos and pulsations. Take a single pitch in a comfortable part of your singing range. Using the vowel *ah,* first pulsate the tone in a succession of *ah-ah-ah-ah-ah-ah'*s, without ever completely stopping the tone until your breath is depleted. Then, after a good inhalation, follow immediately with a succession of staccato *ha/ha/ha/ha/ha/ha'*s (the aspirated *h* will assure a complete stoppage of the tone). Continue to alternate back and forth from pulsation to staccato at approximately the same speed of oscillation until you feel that you are gaining mastery of the coordination of both techniqes. Although many of the muscular processes are very similar, the sensations you experience while performing the exercises may be quite different. For most singers, in the staccato exercise the muscular activity feels as if it were taking place mostly in the thoracic area, perhaps near the bottom of the rib cage. The pulsation exercise feels as if it originated somewhat lower, primarily in the abdominal muscles. In reality, of course, all of the breathing-for-singing muscle groups are involved to some extent in both exercises. However, isolation of the muscles and muscle groups required to execute these two exercises in a controlled fashion will help you achieve the mastery of breathing coordination that is essential to beautiful singing.

POSTURE

The experienced operatic or musical comedy singer performing a physically active role amply demonstrates that no single posture is required for highly successful singing. However, in the early stages of developing singing skills, good posture is a valuable aid. It provides the conditions necessary to allow the entire singing apparatus to function most freely and effectively. In addition, establishing good habits of posture while learning to sing will likely give you a pleasing physical appearance when the time for actual performance arrives.

An ideal singing posture is one that allows you to breathe, produce well-supported tone, and recover your breath in the most comfortable and tension-free manner possible. For solo singing a standing position is most common, whereas in choral singing a considerable amount of singing is done while seated, especially during rehearsals. You will want to become equally comfortable and efficient singing in either position eventually, but at first you will probably find the standing position the easiest in which to learn correct posture.

Correct body alignment for singing is the goal of good posture. Only when the body is correctly aligned can the singer attain the balance needed for maximum vocal efficiency. If certain parts of the body are misaligned, other parts must move out of line to maintain balance and counteract the effect of gravity. Rounded shoulders, the neck arched too far forward or downward, a collapsed rib cage, the spine in either a swayback position or a slouch arching forward, all the body weight pitched awkwardly on one leg, and so forth, are all manifestations of poor posture, resulting in incorrect body alignment for singing. These conditions not only waste energy but also put the body in positions that inhibit all aspects of vocal production—from breathing to resonance. In addition, poor body alignment is fundamentally linked with a sense of lethargy, a lack of poise, and even a poor self-image.

When your body assumes a correct posture for singing you will feel an unmistakable sense of alertness, balance, and poise. Looking at yourself in a full-length mirror is the most important aid you can use to help achieve this condition. Your head should sit comfortably high on your spine, almost as if suspended from above. Your chin should point neither up nor down, but in a relaxed, confident, straight-ahead position. Your chest should be held high, but comfortably so, without tension. It, and your shoulders, should not heave noticeably up and down when you breathe in and out. Your abdominal region should be relaxed but not flaccid, firm but not tense. It should be consciously relaxed each time you inhale. Your back should be straight but not rigid; avoid a swayback stance at all costs—it virtually assures inhibited breathing. Your hips should be rolled somewhat forward so that your tailbone is tucked in slightly. Keep your knees flexible and as relaxed as possible. Discreetly shifting some of your weight from one leg to the other from time to time helps avoid tension and fatigue. Your feet should be neither too close together nor awkwardly far apart; keep a comfortable distance between them. An easy balance can be achieved by placing one foot slightly ahead of the other. By all means put the weight of the body on the balls of your feet, never on the heels. Such a stance looks alert and assertive and gives you a confident sense of balance. This leaves only the arms and hands, which usually have little to do with actual singing but much to do with your appearance. The most important consideration is that they be relaxed and comfortable. Assume a natural, relaxed position with them simply hanging at your sides, unless you wish to rest your right hand on the piano (assuming you are singing in front of a grand). Avoid clasping your hands affectedly in front of you or holding them behind your back, and don't put them in your pockets.

The sensations of balance, poise, and energy should be much the same if you are seated. Sit away from the back of the chair, with both feet on the floor. If you are holding music, hold it high enough so you don't have to look down, constricting the larynx and restricting the free flow of breath. Whether standing or seated be sure that none of your clothing (belt, necktie, collar with high buttons, and so forth) in any way restricts your breathing or impairs your singing posture.

CLASSROOM EXERCISES

The breathing exercises and techniques suggested above are to be practiced individually on a daily basis until you master them thoroughly. Even after coordination is achieved, consistent practice (perhaps on a reduced scale) will continue to develop and reinforce your breathing technique and breath support skills. Toward this end these exercises should be maintained to some degree throughout the course. In addition, the following exercises are suggested, to be introduced during the class sessions. They may first be practiced together (the group effort sometimes makes them easier to grasp quickly), and later these too may be incorporated into your regular individual practice routine.

Since the following vocalises involve the use of specific pitches, the instructor will probably assist the class from the piano. First the instructor will check the class one by one for individual mastery of both the *staccato* and the *pulsation* techniques. Then, for a brief warm-up and memory refresher, the class should sing Exercise 2.1 together. Following this, the instructor should check each student individually to be sure the staccato is completely detached, the attack is clean and free of breathiness, and so forth. Each student should be appraised of his or her success with the technique or need for further work.

Exercise 2.1   *Single-tone staccato*

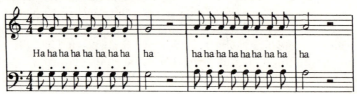

Ha ha ha ha ha ha ha ha   ha   ha ha ha ha ha ha ha ha   ha

ha ha ha ha ha ha ha ha   ha   ha ha ha ha ha ha ha ha   ha   (Etc.)

Repeat exercise beginning one half-step higher each time.

Next the class together should practice Exercise 2.2 at a tempo accessible to everyone in the group. Both the students and the instructor observing the students should pay attention to breathing and support mechanisms.

When the staccato technique seems to be at least clearly *understood* by every member of the class, even if not totally mastered, a pulsation vocalise may be introduced. The simple, single-pitch one in Exercise 2.3 should be done first, by the class together and then individually—to be sure everyone has achieved the basic coordination. Some members of the class probably will not have mastered the technique by this class meeting; they may receive considerable assistance from demonstrations by both the instructor and other members of the class who have developed correct coordination more quickly. The instructor must be sure that the pulsation is continuous and that the tone is never interrupted prior to the rest, either by an *h* or by a *glottal stop.*[2]

---

2. The glottal stop is a sudden termination of the tone accomplished by closing the glottis against the airflow, resulting in an abrupt, unpleasant choking-off of the tone. A demonstration by the instructor will clarify this undesirable technique. Glottal attacks are also possible, and are sometimes acceptable, particularly in speech. Both glottal attacks and releases are discussed in Chapter 3.

Exercise 2.2 *Staccato scale*

Continue by half-steps to G; then descend by half-steps back to C.

Exercise 2.3 *Single-tone pulsation*

Return down to G, then raise sequence a half-step and repeat.

At the appropriate time, the class should then practice Exercise 2.4. The ability to coordinate this exercise will undoubtedly vary greatly among students. Those who have difficulty at first should not despair but should spend some extra time working on this technique in private practice. Sometimes it is helpful if two or three students who need such extra practice arrange a few sessions together.

Exercise 2.4 *Pulsation scale*

Continue by half-steps to G; then descend by half-steps back to C.

Exercise 2.5, deceptively simple in appearance, is another valuable device for learning to develop skillful breath *control*. It is important to sing each three measures on a single breath; then the breath recovery must be of full capacity, making use of all inhalation muscles. The instructor should demonstrate the exercise to the class first, then all students should practice it together. Finally each class member should be heard individually. The

Exercise 2.5 *Crescendo-decrescendo*

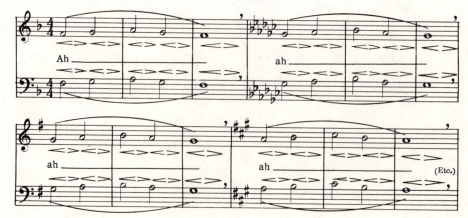

evenness of both the crescendo and the decrescendo should be carefully monitored. Acquiring skill in regulating the consistency of volume change will develop the *control* desired.[3]

ASSIGNMENTS

1. Practice all breathing exercises and breath control vocalises in this chapter daily. Notice and appreciate the progress you make in achieving coordination of the muscles involved.

2. Read Chapter 3 and practice all the exercises suggested (except the Classroom Exercises—some of these may require a demonstration or further explanation from your instructor).

3. Continue to prepare the song you selected. You should be ready to perform it by the conclusion of the next chapter.

---

3. An occasional student may have some difficulty with most of the breathing and support exercises mentioned in this chapter (both those for individual practice and those for classroom activity) because his or her support muscles are "out of shape." If the student is physically inactive, overweight, or in poor physical condition for some other reason, conventional physical exercises such as sit-ups and leg raises are recommended in addition to the vocal exercises specified above.

3

PHONATION

THE PRODUCTION OF SINGING TONE

Many great singers have confessed ignorance about how the voice works; probably more have revealed it without confessing, when asked about physiological matters. Jenny Lind, one of the world's famous singers in the late nineteenth century, is said to have remarked that the secret to her unusual success was that she sang with her uvula![1] Kirsten Flagstad, considered by many the greatest soprano of this century, stated that she had no idea why her voice behaved as it did. Singing, she said, simply came as naturally to her as breathing.[2] Must you understand the functions of the various parts of the singing mechanism to sing well? It is certainly true that birds need not understand the functions of their wings (let alone know the names of the muscles and bones in them) in order to fly successfully. Certainly *some* singers learn to skillfully perform with

1. Ernest G. White, *Sinus Tone Production* (Boston: Crescendo Publishing Co., 1950), p. 17.

2. Judith Litante, *A Natural Approach to Singing* (Dubuque, Iowa: Wm. C. Brown, 1959), p. 1.

very little understanding of how they do it. But, even for these, increased knowledge of how the singing instrument functions would more than likely enable them to sing with greater skill and beauty; it would certainly help them to protect and maintain their voices throughout their careers. There is no doubt that the beginning singer, perhaps not endowed with natural coordination, can benefit greatly from some understanding of the singing organs. Knowing how the voice functions is a great aid in acquiring control of it.

If you place your fingertips on your "Adam's apple" (the front, or anterior, portion of your larynx) and sing a tone, you will feel a slight vibration. This is where your singing tone originates. Two slender bands of tissue inside this voice box, vibrating in such a way as to emit the air from the lungs in regular, controlled "puffs," initiate the sound we call singing. The next time you hear the great operatic voice of a Joan Sutherland or a Placido Domingo, consider that the origin of all of that rich, powerful tone is in two tiny vocal "lips" less than one inch long.[3] How do these vocal lips, or cords, function to produce singing tone? Prior to the production of tone, the vocal cords are closed. But they are highly elastic and flexible, so, when the singer allows a column of air from the lungs to be expelled against them, they open slightly, allowing a tiny puff of air to escape. They then close immediately, opening again to allow another puff to escape, in a continuous cycle. How fast or slow these cycles of puffs are emitted determines the pitch of the vocal sound. Even as infants, we learn almost instinctively to adjust our vocal cords to bring about these pitch changes.

Like the breathing process, phonation (the production of tone) is an incredibly complex process, and we have only limited conscious control over parts of it. We can control much of it, however, and we can *train* our voices to respond to this control with considerable coordination and sophistication. Before exploring these possibilities, it will be helpful for you to study some illustrations of the vocal apparatus. See Figures 3.1 and 3.2. Although it is not necessary to memorize all the complicated names of parts of the vocal anatomy in order to learn to sing well, the parts are carefully labeled here so you can distinguish one from another and understand how each functions in the singing process.

THE PHYSIOLOGY OF PHONATION

When breath is expelled from the lungs, the air passes through the bronchial tubes into the *trachea* (or windpipe), where it is funneled into the *larynx*,[4] sometimes called the *voice box*. It is within this incredibly complex structure of cartilage and muscle tissue that vocal tone originates. The primary function of the larynx, however, is not singing, but housing one of the body's most important *valves*. This valve is actually comprised of the vocal cords themselves, and its *main* purpose is to keep foreign matter (such as food and drink) from entering the lungs and to stop inhalation or exhalation. It happens that humans have also learned to use the valve to speak and to make beautiful music.

---

3. The average length in men is about nine-tenths of an inch; in women, about seven-tenths.
4. The word is pronounced *lehr-inks* and not *lehr-nix* as, unfortunately, even some trained singers say it.

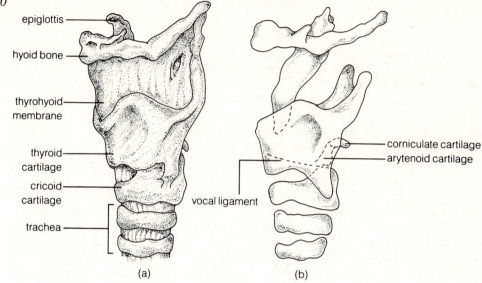

Figure 3.1   Cartilaginous structure of the larynx
*These illustrations are side views, from the left, showing the external cartilages
(a) and internal structures (b).*

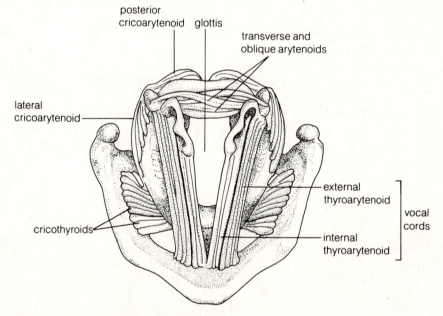

Figure 3.2   Musculature of the larynx
This illustration is a cross section of the larynx, looking down.

If you lift a heavy weight, the *glottis* (the opening of the "valve") automatically
closes. To test this statement, try keeping the glottis open (for example, exhale) while
lifting a heavy object. What happens? It is as if your body had collapsed; you have
no strength. At one time or another in your life you have probably suffered the

consequences of swallowing something "down the wrong pipe." This was an instance when the valve didn't close in time, and you had to cough until the foreign substance was forced out of the trachea.

The larynx is so complicated a structure that it is not possible to observe all its functional parts at once. Therefore we will look first at the cartilaginous portions that form its "skeleton." Look back at Figure 3.1. The larynx is connected to the trachea beneath it by the *cricoid cartilage,* which is the uppermost ring of the trachea. Above the cricoid is the largest cartilage, the *thyroid cartilage;* you can easily feel its distinctive wedge shape with your thumb and forefinger. Above the thyroid and at the top of the larynx is the *hyoid bone,* the only real bone in the larynx; you can feel the front tip of it if you place a finger just above the point of your Adam's apple. Inside the larynx, attached to the front, is a leaf-shaped flap of cartilage called the *epiglottis.* It forms a protective cover over the vocal cords during the swallowing process—a kind of lid over the valve. It adds a measure of protection in keeping foreign objects from entering the breathing area. The remaining cartilages of the larynx are also inside, just above the cricoid ring. They consist of two matched pairs. The *arytenoids* are connected to the thyroid by the *vocal ligaments* (which outline the inside edges of the glottal opening). Directly above these are the two matching *corniculates,* which work in tandem with the arytenoids.

All of the cartilages of the larynx are held together by ligaments, giving the entire structure a great deal of flexibility. To get an idea of how much movement is possible, place your fingertips on your larynx and swallow. What happens? A number of activities take place on the inside, but on the outside you can feel everything below the hyoid bone move up significantly and then move back to the normal position after the swallow is completed.

The musculature of the larynx is even more interesting than its cartilaginous structure, because the tissue vibration that produces vocal sound occurs in muscles. The muscles of the larynx are even more numerous and complex than the cartilages. For the sake of simplicity we will concentrate on only those most directly involved with singing.

Of course, the most significant singing muscles are those we call the *vocal cords.*[5] There are *two* matched pairs of muscles that make up the cords, a thick outside set called the *external thyroarytenoid* muscles (because they are connected to the thyroid cartilage at one end and to the arytenoid cartilage at the other) and a thinner inside set attached to the vocal ligaments called the *internal thyroarytenoid* muscles (also sometimes called the *vocalis* muscles). The action of these muscles sets up the vibrations that produce the sound we call singing. How do they work?

The process is not a simple one. These tiny, remarkable muscles are able to change rapidly in tension, length, and thickness. This is accomplished by their own contraction (altering thickness) and by the action of other intrinsic muscles also attached to the arytenoid cartilages. The *cricoarytenoid* muscles cause the arytenoids to rotate, changing both their length and tension. The *transverse* and *oblique arytenoid* muscles cause the cords to come together or part, opening and closing the glottis. The com-

5. Vocal *cords* has long been considered misleading terminology because it suggests *strings* of some type. Vocal *bands* is sometimes used; vocal *folds* is an even more common term. Probably the most accurate descriptive term is vocal *lips,* for in function and appearance they resemble lips more than anything else.

bined action of all these tiny muscles, along with the energy supplied by the breath, enables the potentially simple valve we spoke of earlier to *phonate*—and to do so with a fascinating array of possibilities. As a result of this tiny, but highly complex muscular activity, the voice can (1) start or stop tone (attack and release), (2) change pitch, (3) change volume, or loudness (aided by breath control), and (4) change timbre, or tone color (aided by resonance, discussed in Chapter 4).

ATTACK AND RELEASE

Figure 3.3 shows the glottis closed (a) and open (b). For breathing, it must be open; for lifting heavy weights and for performing certain body functions, including swallowing, it must be closed. For singing (and speaking), it assumes a position that *looks* closed to the naked eye, but in actuality it is opening slightly and then closing in a rapid vibration, emitting exhaled air in the regular, controlled puffs mentioned earlier. This produces a musical tone (or a speech sound). Initiation of a tone is called the *attack;* its termination is referred to as the *release.*

There are three basic ways to execute a vocal attack: *aspirated, glottal,* and *co-ordinated.* The aspirated attack is the result of preceding any vowel sound with a puff

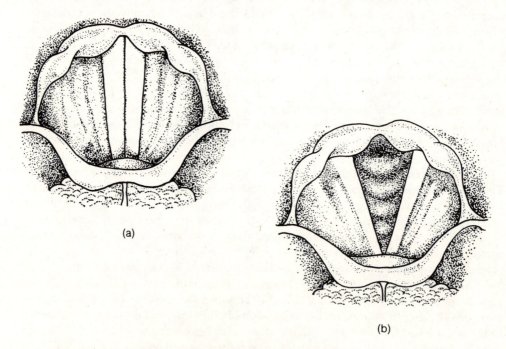

(a)

(b)

**Figure 3.3   Position of the vocal cords during
phonation (a) and at rest (b)**
The glottis (the opening between the cords) is closed during swallowing or lifting heavy weights and open during normal breathing. During phonation the cords appear to the eye as shown in (a), but they actually open slightly and close in a rapid vibratory pattern.

of unvocalized air, as in the consonant *h* (*ha, ho, hey,* and so forth). If, in singing, an *h* sound is heard but is not intended, it is simply a case of the breath escaping before the glottis gets closed, and we term this attack "breathy" (with negative connotations). The glottal attack is the result of opening the glottis too *late*. As a consequence a slight pressure is built up below the larynx, and when it is finally opened the sound emerges in a slight "explosion."[6] This kind of attack is almost always to be avoided in singing (due to its rather crude, unattractive sound), except occasionally in highly emotional operatic situations, and even then its appropriateness is questioned by many. (Its use in speech, however, is not unusual or necessarily offensive.) The most common singing attack is one in which the release of breath and the closure of the glottis are coordinated, such as in a quiet initiation of the vowel *ah*.

It is important for beginning singers to learn to produce a coordinated attack, for the attack has a close relationship to development of the overall vocal technique. To understand how to do an act, it is often helpful to compare the correct method with an incorrect one. To put this axiom into practice yourself, first execute a series of aspirated attacks (these are not always incorrect, certainly, but often to be avoided): *ha-ha-ha-ha-ha.* Do this at different pitch levels, different volume levels, and different speeds. Then substitute glottal attacks (another demonstration may be necessary). Finally do a series of normal, coordinated attacks in the same way. Again try different vowels, different volume levels, and different speeds. Notice carefully the differences in both the sensations of producing the three kinds of attacks and the way the three sound. The most important result is to gain a coordinated attack that is really *coordinated.* When you have acquired this skill (you may very well have it already), your attacks will be smooth, quiet, and (the ultimate attribute) unnoticeable.

There are also three possible ways to release a tone, and they can be given the same names: *aspirated, glottal,* and *coordinated.* However, in the release, the aspirated and glottal versions are *never* acceptable in singing. If you stop the tone before you stop the breath, you will get: *ah-h-h-h-h.* Try it. Your voice will sound as if it had suddenly sprung a leak. If you close the glottis before you stop the breath, you will get: *ah-H/.* There will be a sudden and unpleasant "thud" as the tone stops. The only correct and musically acceptable way to end a tone is the *coordinated* release, with the tone and the breath terminating at exactly the same time. Accomplishing this may at first sound difficult, but you have probably been doing it for a long time without realizing it.

To distinguish clearly among the three possibilities of attack and release and to be sure you are using only the coordinated release, try all three types one after another. First an aspirated attack and release sequence: *haaaah-h-h-h, haaaah-h-h-h, haaaah-h-h-h.* (Repeat substituting different vowels.) Now attack and release with a glottal stroke: *Aaaaah-H/, Aaaaah-H/, Aaaaah-H/.*[7] (Again use different vowels as well.)

---

6. Since the actual sound of the glottal attack is somewhat difficult to describe accurately, a demonstration by the instructor will probably clarify it most effectively.

7. If executed with fairly rapid repetitions, the sequence will sound somewhat like the bark of a seal! While not very musical-sounding, it *is* the basis for a very effective exercise to help solve certain vocal problems.

Finally use the *coordinated* technique for both the attack and the release—the correct means of producing tones in the great majority of singing: *aaah, aaah, aaah.*

CHANGING PITCH, VOLUME, AND TIMBRE

Changes in pitch, volume, and timbre (tone quality, the distinctive "color" of the tone) also have their origin, at least to some degree, in the phonation process. However, they are also affected considerably by both breath and resonance. The primary factor in changing *pitch* in the voice is the ability of the vocal cords to change in length, tension, and thickness, as mentioned earlier. This is a highly complex process, involving a number of tiny muscular activities in the larynx. Changes in the length and tension of the cords are accomplished by stretching or slackening them: (1) the thyroid cartilage rocks forward on its tiny hinges (called the *inferior cornu*), and (2) the arytenoid cartilage rotates. Since the vocal cords are attached to the thyroid cartilage in the front and the arytenoids in the back, these movements cause the cords to stretch or slacken. The thickness of the cords is changed by contraction or relaxation of the thyroarytenoid muscles. These changes in length, tension, and thickness of the vocal cords result in change of pitch; the greater the tension and the thinner the mass of the muscle, the faster the puffs of air will emerge and the higher the pitch will be. However, leading voice scientists agree that the air pressure in the trachea (as supplied by breath support) has a definite effect on pitch as well.

Of course this tracheal air pressure has a primary effect on *volume.* The greater the pressure the greater the sound. However, loudness is also affected greatly by resonance, or amplification due to sympathetic vibration in the body's resonators, a topic that will be enlarged upon in Chapter 4. *Timbre* may be more directly affected by the action of resonance than by what takes place in the phonation process, but most authorities believe that many tone-quality characteristics do originate in the vocal cords. The particular way a given set of vocal cords lengthens and shortens, thins and thickens, tenses and relaxes undoubtedly affects that voice's unique "color." Also, there is no doubt that the structure of the vocal apparatus—the specific size and shape of the larynx and everything it contains—predetermines to a large degree what the timbral possibilities will be.

POSITION OF THE LARYNX

Remember the experiment we did of placing a fingertip upon the larynx while swallowing? You noticed that the larynx moved up, returning to its normal position when the process was completed. You probably were not aware that the glottis closed too, while you were swallowing. The swallowing process is executed not by the intrinsic muscles of the larynx that we have examined in this chapter but by *extrinsic* laryngeal muscles—those lying outside the larynx. Thus, the singing and swallowing processes are isolated from one another. Swallowing is, in fact, an enemy of correct singing technique; if the swallowing muscles are even slightly engaged, they interfere substantially with the singing process. Notice that you cannot sing at all when you are actually swallowing, even if you are swallowing no substance.

Place your fingertip on your larynx again and now sing a one-octave, ascending scale, starting on a moderately low pitch (C, perhaps). Does your larynx move up as the pitches get higher? Or does it perhaps rise only on the last few pitches? If it doesn't move at all, good! This means that, at these pitch levels at least, you have little or no interference from the swallowing muscles. If you did notice substantial movement of the larynx, your swallowing muscles are unconsciously engaging, causing the singing process to compete against the much stronger swallowing process. The result is undue vocal strain, which can eventually cause vocal injury. In fact, if your larynx moved up substantially, the highest notes of your scale probably sounded pinched and felt strained.

How can this engagement of the swallowing muscles be avoided? By *conscious relaxation* of these muscles. Return to your one-octave scale, keeping your fingertip touching your larynx, but this time avail yourself of a good mirror. As you ascend the scale watch the larynx. If it begins to rise, try consciously to "relax it down." Don't attempt to *force* it down, internally or externally. Manually holding it down will produce no lasting benefits either. You may have to make several tries, but eventually the point at which your larynx begins to rise will occur higher and higher in the scale, giving you a substantially increased upper range, free of tension. The more firmly entrenched your prior habit of engaging the swallowing muscles on high pitches, the longer it will take to unlearn. The relaxed, unraised position of the larynx is absolutely essential to good vocal production, and it spares the singing muscles unnecessary wear, tear, and strain. If it takes a while to master conscious relaxation of the swallowing muscles, it is well worth the patience required; you are learning to improve and protect the only voice you will ever have.

CLASSROOM EXERCISES

As suggested in Chapter 2, all of the practice devices and exercises given in this chapter should be executed (and repeated until mastered) before you attend the first class session devoted to phonation. If you have questions or need demonstrations from the instructor, take care of these matters before you attempt the Classroom Exercises. *You need to understand the concepts presented before you can apply them to a productive practice routine.* You will probably assimilate the vocalises presented in the Classroom Exercises most efficiently if they are demonstrated by the instructor. When the exercises are executed by the class as a whole the first time, reinforcement and "leading" with a piano are essential.

The class should practice the exercises together for a time; then each member should sing them individually. Afterward they may be incorporated into each student's regular practice routine, with special attention given to the ones that cause the most difficulty. In addition to their primary value of teaching the concepts of attack and release, all of the exercises presented here serve as excellent vocal warm-ups for the more demanding vocalises of any practice session.

Exercise 3.5 *Pulsation technique with staccato release*

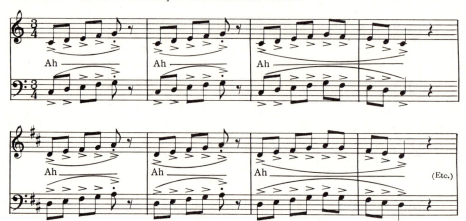

ASSIGNMENTS

1. Add the exercises and vocalises in this chapter (particularly any that give you trouble) to your breathing exercises and breath control vocalises from Chapter 2. Monitor, and appreciate, your progress.

2. Read Chapter 4, and practice all the exercises except the Classroom Exercises.

3. At the conclusion of this chapter you should be prepared for your first real performance before the class. Remember that it is just that—a *first* performance. This early in the course many techniques and skills are yet to be presented and mastered, so the performance is not expected to be a finished product. But do your best singing, using the information presented thus far, along with your prior singing skills. Take advantage of the vocal progress you've already made, and know that much more lies ahead.

4. After you have completed your first performance for the class, you probably will wish to adjust your preparation technique for your next song. Some things probably need a bit more attention; others that concerned you before you performed turned out to be no problem at all. Note these considerations as you prepare your next song. Suggestions:

    a. "Black Is the Color of My True Love's Hair," pages 152–159.
    b. "He's Gone Away," pages 172–173.

4

RESONATION

SELECTIVE AMPLIFICATION OF SINGING TONE

What is resonance? When applied to the voice, resonance is the process of selective amplification of components of the vocal tone, which originates in the larynx, by the vocal resonators. These resonators consist of two types: surfaces and cavities. Surface resonance includes the reflection of vibrations and the sympathetic vibration of matter connected to or surrounding a vibrating body, such as a sounding board. In the voice the materials for surface resonance are the bones and flesh of the body near the voice box, from the chest to the head. While its existence cannot be discounted, surface resonance is not of much interest to the singer, for most of it cannot be controlled. It is important only in that it creates sensations that the singer can feel and learn to identify with either good or poor vocal production.

Cavity resonance, in contrast, is

substantially controllable. In the voice, as in other musical instruments, resonating cavities are filled with air. Movement of this air, propelled by pulsations by the vibrator (vocal cords), is modified in the resonating cavity. How this motion of the air, with its properties of elasticity and mass, is reinforced (or weakened) is determined by the volume of the cavity, the size of the openings in and out of the cavity, and the texture (soft and absorbent, or hard and reflective) of the walls of the cavity. The significant areas of cavity resonance over which we have considerable control are in the throat, the mouth, and the nasal cavities.

The amplification provided by our resonators is selective in that certain components (called *overtones*) of the original sound produced by the vocal cords are strengthened more than others. Some are dampened or weakened, and the resultant tone possesses a distinctive quality or *timbre*. Differences in timbre are the characteristics that differentiate the sounds of different instruments or voices. To understand how this process works, it is first necessary to understand a few principles of musical acoustics and the theory of harmonic overtones.

If a violinist draws a bow across a string, or a pianist depresses a key on the piano, a string, in both cases, is set into vibration. Should the frequency of that vibration happen to be 440 cycles per second, our ears interpret the pitch as A (above middle C). Yet the two musical tones sound distinctively different. Why? Because the violin and the piano possess different timbres or "colors" of tone. Although our ears identify the basic vibration of 440 cycles per second, the strings of both the piano and the violin are also oscillating in subvibrations (multiples of the fundamental vibration) called *harmonic overtones* or *harmonic partials*. To explore this premise, seat yourself at a piano and silently (without letting the hammers strike the strings) depress as many keys with your right hand and arm as you can in an area near the middle of the keyboard. This releases the dampers on all of those strings, allowing them to vibrate freely. Now, while holding the keys down, strike a single note below those keys with your left hand, and *release it immediately*. What do you hear? If you listen carefully you will hear a combination of pitches. The overtones from the note you struck with your left hand have caused certain of the strings to vibrate sympathetically. The strings that vibrate are those in tune with the pitches of the overtones. This experiment demonstrates the subvibrations (overtones) that exist within all musical tones, in addition to the fundamental frequency of that tone. Although our ears do not usually analyze the specific pitches of the overtones, they do respond to the tone quality (timbre) of the composite of fundamental and overtones, so that we can easily distinguish between the sound of the violin and that of the piano. The relative strength of the specific overtones produced by these very different instruments with their different resonators (sounding boards etc.) accounts for the marked difference in quality between the tones produced by each.

What causes overtones and variance in their intensities among musical instruments and voices? Harmonic overtones occur in nature in a predictable series. Figure 4.1 shows the order of the series for the pitch two octaves below middle C. For every tone-producing medium, the relative strength of these overtones is unique. To further illustrate this phenomenon, the timbres of the oboe and the French horn are compared in Figure 4.2. The shapes of the two graphs reveal a difference in strength and weakness of various overtones indicative of the great difference between the timbres of these two instruments. Of course, the graphs would vary slightly even between two oboes, or two French horns, but only slightly, because the size, shape, pitch range,

Figure 4.1   The harmonic overtone series

It should be noted that, except in the case of octaves, the harmonic partials are not exactly in tune with the notes of the scale in our present system of tuning. The scale tones written here most nearly approximate the pitches of the true harmonics.

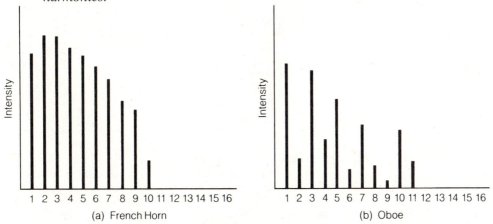

Figure 4.2   Harmonic overtone intensity pattern (sound recipe) for the French horn (a) and the oboe (b)

Note that the pure, mellow tone quality produced by the French horn is reflected by the rather smooth contour of overtone intensities, while the oboe's complex, reedy tone creates a sharply jagged contour.

and so forth, of the like instruments is essentially the same. In human voices the difference between any two sopranos, baritones, or the like, is much greater because human vocal instruments differ much more in size, shape, pitch range, and so forth, than manufactured oboes or French horns. Hence, just as no one else has a voice constructed exactly like yours, so your vocal timbre is absolutely unique. The purpose of learning about vocal resonance is to take advantage of the unique properties of your voice. You can reinforce and enrich its properties by applying conscious control over your body's resonating abilities. Limitations exist, to be sure, over conscious control of resonance. However, application of the information in this chapter may very well bring more dramatic improvement in your vocal tone than any other single portion of this course. Before learning how to exert control over this aspect of the voice, like other aspects, you need to learn the functions of the anatomical parts involved.

THE PHYSIOLOGY OF RESONANCE

Figure 4.3 provides a clear view of where most vocal resonance takes place. The primary resonance tract is the pharyngeal cavity. It is usually divided into three

memorize for a quiz

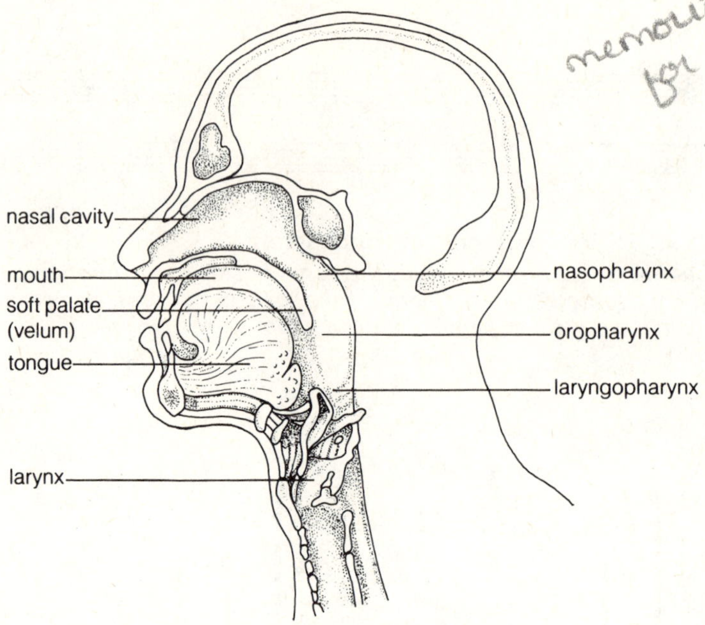

Figure 4.3   Primary areas of vocal resonance
*Lower frequencies are amplified and enhanced primarily in the laryngopharynx,
while the oropharynx is the primary area of resonance for most speech sounds
and middle-range singing tones. The nasopharynx provides the primary resonator for amplifying not only the high singing tones but also the overtones for
lower pitches.*

basic areas of resonation: the *laryngopharynx,* the *oropharynx,* and the *nasopharynx.*
Less important to a singer, because they are not under conscious control and because
their contribution to resonance is debatable, are the *potential* resonators: the tra-
cheobronchial tree (lungs, trachea, and bronchi) and the laryngeal cavities (immediately above and below the glottis).

Although comprised of three separate, individually controlled units, your pharyngeal resonator system functions as an integrated whole when coordinated properly, enabling you to sing over a wide pitch range with remarkable balance of volume
and timbre. Gaining the control required for this coordination necessitates understanding the action and function of each segment of the system.

The laryngopharynx is a muscular, tubelike opening extending from the top of
the larynx to the posterior base of the tongue, where it becomes continuous with the
oropharynx. It is approximately four to five inches long and its walls are smooth and
pliable. This resonator is not highly adjustable, but contraction and relaxation of the
constrictor muscles that comprise the tube can reduce or enlarge the diameter of the
cavity to some degree. The length of the cavity can also be altered by raising or
lowering the larynx.

The oropharynx is the continuation of the pharynx behind the mouth plus the
oral cavity itself, extending up to the soft palate. It is the most adjustable in size and
shape of all the resonance chambers, due to the radical changes produced by the
tongue, lips, sides of the mouth, and so forth. The front wall of the oropharynx is the

back of the tongue; this alone allows significant adjustability. The size and shape of the chamber are also altered dramatically by lowering and raising the jaw. It is possible to close off most oropharynx resonance (rendering actual *singing* impossible) by pressing the back of the tongue firmly against the soft palate, as you do in saying *ng*. The result is one way of humming.

The nasopharynx chamber comprises all the area immediately above the soft palate, including the two nasal cavities. It also has a "door," the soft palate, that can alter the size and shape of the opening to the chamber by rising or lowering and can close the cavity entirely. The only other means of adjusting this cavity is by dilating or relaxing the nostrils. Closing the soft palate (pressing the velum firmly against the pharyngeal wall) effectively eliminates all nasopharynx resonance, with a substantial loss of richness of timbre in the vocal tone and greater difficulty amplifying higher pitches.

HOW THE VOCAL RESONATORS FUNCTION

An analogy can be drawn between the behavior of the resonating system of the human voice and that of a three-way high-fidelity loudspeaker. (It is admittedly an oversimplified and perhaps not entirely scientific analogy.) This kind of speaker, found in good quality stereo systems, consists of a "woofer," a "mid-range driver," and a "tweeter." The woofer reproduces the lower frequencies; the mid-range driver handles the middle tones; the highest notes and the overtones of many lower pitches are reproduced by the tweeter. In the human vocal resonating system, the lowest pitches are resonated most effectively in the laryngopharynx; mid-range notes (and much of the speaking-voice range) resonate efficiently in the oropharynx and (less so) in the mouth; the highest pitches and overtones of lower pitches are amplified most efficiently in the nasopharynx. Unfortunately there is not universal agreement among voice scientists or voice teachers on the function of the nasopharynx in vocal resonance. Some, in fact, advocate avoidance of conscious resonation there altogether, suggesting that a nasal tone quality results. This idea, however, is about as sensible as switching off the tweeter on your stereo speaker to get a better sound. On the contrary, vocal tone well-resonated in the nasopharynx is far richer in quality and beauty than tone produced without nasopharynx resonance. Perhaps more important, it is easier to produce higher pitches when the nasopharynx cavities are used for amplification. Like a fine loudspeaker, the vocal resonance system, when coordinated and trained to function efficiently, produces vocal tone that is rich in timbre and consistent in quality from low notes to high. In the untrained voice, such sophisticated behavior of the resonance system is unlikely. Training the resonators is necessary. To train the muscles and nerves involved you must learn how to control them.

CONTROLLING RESONANCE

If you have ever removed the mouthpiece from a wind instrument—say a trumpet or a clarinet—and blown into it in the usual fashion, you were probably surprised at how feeble the sound was. The fact is that in removing the mouthpiece from the instrument you removed nearly all the instrument's resonating capabilities. Likewise, if the human voice box were taken out of its body enclosure (such experiments have been done with the larynxes of animals), the quality and quantity of its sound-producing ability would be reduced significantly. But situated as it is, connected to the vocal resonating system, it is a highly efficient instrument. A single, well-developed human voice, without artificial amplification, can easily be heard over an entire symphony orchestra and a large chorus. How is this possible? It is done by training the resonating system to amplify, reinforce, and enrich the vocal tone in the most effective manner attainable. It is not an easy process, nor can it usually be accomplished in a short time. It is primarily an activity of memorizing sensations, and much of the early learning involves trial and error. But it is encouraging to know that, once acquired, vocal resonance skills are learned for good. It is much like learning to ride a bicycle or to roller-skate; once you have learned, you will retain the ability even if you abandon the activity for a very long time.[1]

How do you learn to resonate more effectively? There is probably no other aspect of singing in which *imagination* is more important than in learning to resonate well. If you *imagine* focusing your tone, say in your cheekbones, just under your eyes, or even in your forehead, remarkable changes in vocal resonance *can* take place. Sometimes the imagined placement of the tone will "work"—that is, will improve the timbre and power of your voice; sometimes it will not. If it doesn't, this is the point at which a skilled teacher with an exquisitely keen ear is indispensable. More often than not, the beginning singer alone cannot accurately judge either by the sound he or she hears (from the inside) or by the sensations felt, whether a given production of tone is resonated better than another.

Before explaining precisely how to control all possible aspects of your vocal resonating system, let us explore some immediate potentialities. Inhale deeply with a profound yawn. Maintain this feeling in your mouth and throat while singing *ah* on a note low in your range. How does this compare with your usual quality of tone? Now *hum* a note in the upper part of your singing range. After establishing the humming sensation firmly in your mind, open your mouth and sing the same pitch, *while maintaining all the sensations of the hummed tone.* Does this feel or sound different from your usual tone quality in that part of your voice? These two examples should give you some idea of the range of possibilities of control you already possess. There is much more potential for control of the resonating system than you might expect; gaining this control and increasing your skill in this area are the subjects of this portion of our study.

When you yawned, part of the physical effect was that you relaxed constrictor muscles in your throat and enlarged the *laryngopharynx* cavity. This provided the conditions for a darker, "hootier," tone quality. If you actually approximated a yawn, the *ah* you sang was probably unacceptably dark, in terms of beautiful singing. If, however, your laryngopharynx normally tends to be somewhat constricted when you sing and the yawn opened it just enough to relax the constrictor muscles and open your throat, you may have noticed an immediate improvement in both the sound and the sensations of your tone. The laryngopharynx may also be adjusted in length by raising and lowering the larynx. However, optimum resonance is usually achieved when the larynx is in its normal, relaxed position. If you find that yours tends to rise

---

1. This statement applies only to vocal resonance, and not to other aspects of singing such as breathing, which must be consciously trained as long as you continue to sing actively.

on high notes (as mentioned in Chapter 3), the control you need to exert here will be keeping it relaxed as you ascend in pitch.

The *oropharynx* area, if we include the mouth, is almost infinitely adjustable. In fact, one of the most common causes for inconsistency in tone production and in "unevenness" of timbre among singers is that too much adjustment takes place here in singing words. In forming all the necessary vowels and consonants, the jaw, tongue, mouth, and lips are almost constantly assuming different shapes. If the singer is resonating or focusing the tone too much in the mouth, the quality (timbre) of the tone is apt to change with each word, or even syllable. While the area immediately back of the tongue is a highly efficient resonating chamber, the mouth is less so. Its walls are soft and absorbent, and the cavity shape is almost constantly changing. The better you can learn to produce and resonate all vowel sounds in the pharynx and the less you use the mouth as a primary resonator, the more consistent the quality of your tone is likely to be. *Consonant* sounds, on the other hand, are produced entirely in the mouth by the tongue, teeth, lips, soft palate, and the like, and need have no effect on the consistency of the vocal timbre. (The articulation of vowels and consonants will be treated in detail in Chapter 6.)

A helpful technique for learning to resonate vowel sounds primarily in the pharynx and not in the mouth is to produce tones while manually supporting your jaw with one of your hands.[2] This helps relax virtually all jaw and mouth tension, while at the same time assisting you in finding an optimum resonating position for the mouth and throat. Drop your jaw normally as if to sing *ah*, and place your thumb and forefinger along the depressions in each cheek caused by the separation of your upper and lower teeth. Your chin should rest in the cupped palm of your hand. Supporting the jaw in this manner, consciously relax all jaw, mouth, and throat muscles. Now produce a tone in the lower part of your range (perhaps a middle C for women, the octave below for men) on the vowel *ŏŏ* (in IPA symbols, presented on pages 64–65, [U]), as in the word "book." Sustain and repeat the tone a few times, being aware of the free, relaxed, and very resonant sensation you feel. Begin the tone again and, without any modification in the position of the larynx, throat, jaw, or mouth, suddenly shift the tone one octave higher, using slightly greater breath support as you move to the high note. If executed correctly, you should feel and hear a decided improvement in the quality of the higher tone from what you have produced in that pitch area before. Experiment with this exercise on the same vowel at other pitch levels for a time (it is an excellent vowel for finding a free, relaxed position for good resonance); then try other vowel sounds. The key to success with this exercise is to depend on the *breath* for achieving the high tone, not on radical adjustments in the mouth and throat. Mastery of the exercise will add power and beauty of tone to your singing that you probably have not experienced before. Of course the ultimate aim of this technique is to learn to produce all vowels in this free, relaxed manner, uncontrived by the mouth, lips, tongue, and so forth, which will allow you the most *consistent* timbre possible. A word of caution: Once you have found this optimum resonance position with the assistance of your hand on the jaw, abandon use of the hand; don't let it become a crutch.

The *nasopharynx* is the least adjustable of the vocal resonators, but certainly not

---

2. I am indebted to Joseph Klein, author of *Singing Technique* (Princeton, N.J.: D. Van Nostrand, 1967), for this technique.

the least important. It is probably the area least used to advantage by many singers, because it is easy to inadvertently close the "door" (the soft palate) to this resonance chamber. Also the soft palate tends to close almost as a reflex when a singer, particularly an inexperienced one, ascends in pitch. Unfortunately this closure directly increases the difficulty of even *producing* the higher tones and causes a deterioration in quality as well—the tone begins to sound tight and pinched.

A simple experiment will indicate whether or not your soft palate closes on high notes. Sing a scale (using the *ah* vowel) that terminates on a note somewhat high in your range—perhaps an E major scale, unless you have a very low voice, in which case perhaps a C major. While sustaining the top note of the scale, place the palm of your hand firmly over your mouth. Does the tone continue as a hum or does it cease, causing a feeling of pressure? If the tone continues into a hum, your soft palate is open; if it stops, or nearly stops, the soft palate "door" is closed (at least partially). If it is closed, try to open it by consciously thinking of the hum. When you are sure it is open and relaxed, maintain the feeling and move your hand from your mouth, continuing to sing. You should now have a free, nasopharynx-resonated tone. It will feel much better to you—much easier to produce—and best of all it will sound more beautiful to your listeners.

A final consideration about learning to control resonance is the use of moderation in each area. If any one resonance cavity is overemphasized, the timbre will suffer. Too much nasal resonance will result in a nasal, twangy quality; too much mouth resonance will render the tone "mouthy" and shallow; too much throat resonance will cause a dull, dark, throaty sound. A keen sense of *balance* in training the resonators is the desired attribute; a vocal tone of ultimate beauty contains a balance of both "bright" and "dark" qualities. Your instructor, your classmates, and your own sensations will help you find this balanced resonance. Skill in maintaining the balance will enable you to sing with the greatest possible beauty and consistency of tone.

CLASSROOM EXERCISES

Before beginning the exercises for this class session, the instructor should be certain each student understands and can execute with some skill the exercises and practice devices presented in this chapter. For some students, demonstration of certain devices will be necessary. Some students may require individual help. Resonance skills usually require considerable time to develop, and these exercises must be practiced thoroughly and consistently throughout the remainder of the course, to derive their benefits.

For best results the exercises should be presented by the instructor, practiced by the class as a whole, and finally sung by each student individually. Once mastered, they should become part of the student's daily practice routine.

Exercise 4.1 is designed to call into action all three basic pharyngeal resonators. It utilizes a nonsense word that is impossible to spell in English. It is pronounced *nyŏŏ* or, in IPA symbols (see pages 64–65), [njU]. Pronounce it by first approximating the *ny* sound in the word "canyon," followed by the vowel *ŏŏ* as in "book." The *n* opens the soft palate, allowing for nasal resonance; the *y* (or [j]), which is really a short *ee*, raises the back of the tongue making ample resonating space in the oropharynx, and the *ŏŏ* vowel is good for opening the laryngopharynx sufficiently for full amplification. The result, if executed properly, is a tone rich in quality, with properties of both brightness and darkness. When you succeed with the exercise, you will probably hear and feel qualities in your voice you have not experienced before. Sing *nyŏŏ* on each descending triad, at a medium loud to loud level to assure the use of enough breath to make the resonance "work." The exercise is deliberately pitched low; it must be sung in the lower register by both male and female voices (registers will be explained in Chapter 5). For the fastest results, hold the jaw as suggested on page 45.

Exercise 4.1   *Descending triad*

The *ee* vowel raises the back of the tongue to its highest position and pulls the bulk of the tongue out of the pharynx. This allows very efficient resonance in the oropharynx. Often an inexperienced singer can first discover the sensations of really efficient vocal resonance with the *ee* vowel, characterized by a distinctive "ring" in the voice. Sing the ascending five-note scale in Exercise 4.2, holding and expanding the top note (increasing its volume slightly); then descend to the original note.

Exercise 4.2   *Five-note scale*

Exercise 4.3 concentrates on laryngopharynx resonance. Hold the jaw gently as before, and sing on the vowel *oh*, approximating a slight yawn. Let the tone sound a bit "woofy," with a very relaxed throat. Particularly endeavor to make the upper octave (second note) feel exactly like the start-

ing pitch, in terms of weight and quality. This will help you learn to avoid engagement of the pharyngeal constrictor muscles on high pitches—a condition that produces a pinched vocal quality. Some teachers call this the "open throat" exercise.

Exercise 4.3 *Ascending octave with descending scale*

One of the best vowels for discovering nasopharynx resonance is a nasal vowel that is common in the French language but less so in English: It is written ɛ̃ (in IPA symbols). You can approximate it by saying the *an* of "ant" without closing on the *n*. When you sing Exercise 4.4, exaggerate that nasality at first, making a "nasty," snarling tone. Even flaring the nostrils will help. This will not render beautiful sounds; quite the contrary, the tone may be decidedly unattractive. But you will discover how to resonate in the nasopharynx, and you can achieve balance later.

Exercise 4.4 *Whole-step oscillation*

*See the International Phonetic Alphabet, Chapter 6.

Finally, using an *ah* vowel, try to incorporate the use of all resonators again in the vocalise in Exercise 4.5. Remember to work for a ringing timbre that has qualities of both brightness and darkness in it throughout the range. This exercise requires a substantial supply of breath!

Exercise 4.5   *Ascending arpeggio with descending scale*

ASSIGNMENTS

1. Add the exercises in this chapter to your daily routine; concentrate particularly on those that seem to present difficulties for you or that you feel you may not totally understand yet. Give yourself the time to benefit from the resonance-building skills they offer you.

2. Read Chapter 5 and experiment with the suggested exercises. These exercises, more than those in prior chapters, may require the supervision of your instructor to make sure you are "getting them right."

3. Begin preparation of a new song. Suggestions:
  a. "O Waly, Waly," pages 190–191.
  b. "Danny Boy," pages 160–167.

5

REGISTRATION

DO YOU HAVE MORE THAN ONE VOICE?

At some time in your life you have probably marveled at a great singer whose voice exhibited a very wide range, from deep low notes to brilliant high ones. One of the things that probably impressed you was the fact that from the lowest note to the highest the singer exhibited the same rich vocal quality—no squeaky tones, no growling tones, and no "seams" where one quality ended and another began. The voice quality was "even" from top to bottom. Many singers, including successful artists (particularly in the popular fields of rock, folk, and country music), do not possess such voices. Their voices may display two, three, or even more distinctly different qualities. You probably have already discovered that your own voice sounds a certain way from its lowest pitches up to a certain point; then you feel a "gear shift," and it utterly changes in sound and sensation.

What is this phenomenon, and why doesn't the great singer exhibit it? The great singer's voice is constructed just like everyone else's, including yours. The reason that voice doesn't shift from quality to quality is that, either by natural coordination or by skilled training, the singer has achieved a high level of muscular coordination making it possible to avoid what is called the *register break*.

The register break (Italians call it the *passaggio* or passage) is the point where the untrained voice undergoes an abrupt vibratory change. Literally, what happens is a sudden transition from a thick vibratory mass of muscle tissue to a thinner one that can vibrate faster, producing higher and lighter tones. To understand how the process works, you need to know a bit more about the anatomy of the larynx.

THE PHYSIOLOGY OF REGISTERS

Chapter 3 described how the intrinsic musculature of the larynx is constructed. You may wish to review Figure 3.2. When the voice is at rest, such as during normal breathing, the vocal cords are held apart from each other by the *posterior cricoarytenoid* muscles. When you prepare to speak or sing, the cords are brought together (so that phonation may take place) by the *transverse* and *oblique arytenoid* muscles, an action voice scientists call *medial compression*. The basic muscles of phonation, or the *vibrators*, are the *internal* and *external thyroarytenoids* (commonly known as the *vocal cords*). These vibrating tissues produce the regular, controlled puffs of air that become vocal sound. The primary muscles of pitch are the *cricothyroids*, which exert longitudinal tension on the thyroarytenoids, causing them to vibrate slowly or rapidly, according to the tension.

What, in this highly complicated anatomical structure, *causes* vocal "registers"? Although not every facet of the phenomenon is completely understood, most leading voice scientists agree that vocal registers are the result of the conditions of vibration in the *internal* thyroarytenoids, also known as the *vocalis* muscles.[1] Like all muscles of the body, the vocalis muscles have the ability either to contract or to relax. Contraction of this pair of muscles results in a thickening of the muscle mass; when relaxed, the vocal lips are comparatively thinner. The thicker, contracted muscles form a greater vibrating mass, causing a larger amplitude of movement and slower vibrations. Use of the vocal cords in this state is what most voice professionals call singing in the *lower register* (also often called the "chest voice"). When the vocalis muscles are relaxed, the cricothyroid muscles can exert a greater longitudinal tension on them, forming a smaller, thinner mass. This causes a correspondingly smaller amplitude of movement and faster vibrations. The resultant sound is higher in pitch and lighter in quality. It is usually called the *upper register* (or "head voice"). In the untrained voice the lower and upper registers usually sound distinctly different in timbre from one another. Whichever register the singer has used the most in speech and singing in the past will probably be decidedly stronger than the other, and there will probably be a notable "break" when the singer goes from one to the other—an unpleasant shift that can occur at most inopportune moments during a song. It is encouraging to note, however, that such breaks are seldom exhibited by trained

---

1. William Vennard, *Singing: The Mechanism and the Technique* (New York: Carl Fischer, 1967), pp. 63–64, gives a clear and thorough explanation of this subject.

Figure 5.2   Classifications of vocal ranges and qualities

FEMALE

High Voice Range: **Soprano**

Coloratura soprano — Highest and lightest voice type; capable of great agility and florid singing.

[handwritten: Trudy Suus]

Lyric soprano — Most common soprano type; "lyric" connotes light voice quality.

[handwritten: Elizabeth (sp) Soren tof Black head Schwarzkopf]

Lyrico-spinto soprano — Usually shortened to spinto soprano; heavier and darker quality than lyric, but not as heavy as dramatic.

Dramatic soprano — Largest and heaviest of high female voices; somewhat the quality of mezzo-soprano, but with higher range. Rare category, seldom well developed until middle age.

[handwritten: Birgit Nilsson]

MALE

High Voice Range: **Tenor**

Countertenor — Highest of male voices, also lightest quality; sings above normal tenor range, often in alto or even soprano range. Very uncommon.

[handwritten: Russell Oberlin (messiah) re-inforced falsetto]

Lyric tenor — Comparable to lyric soprano—high range, light quality. Probably most common tenor voice type.

[handwritten: Pavarotti high "c"]

Lyrico-spinto or spinto tenor — Comparable to lyrico-spinto soprano—heavier than lyric, but not as heavy as dramatic.

Dramatic tenor — Like dramatic soprano—large, powerful, almost baritone in quality but capable of high range.

[handwritten: Placido Domingo]

Heldentenor; tenor robusto — Categories for specialized literature; Heldentenor or "heroic" tenor has unusual power and brilliance required in Wagner's operas; robusto is Italian category, equally dramatic and powerful.

have no doubt also heard the term *baritone* and know that it is a medium-low male category, between tenor and bass. You have probably heard the "second soprano" in choral music referred to as a *mezzo-soprano*, the female category between soprano and alto. These six vocal categories provide a fairly accurate classification of all the normal human ranges of pitch. Voices within the same general ranges can differ radically in quality, however, as you have no doubt discovered in listening to your peers in this class. Attempts have been made to classify voices further according to "color" (bright or dark) and/or texture (heavy or light). The *lyrico-spinto* soprano, for instance, is a "middleweight" soprano—neither a "light" nor a "heavy" voice quality; the *basso profundo* is the lowest and darkest of the bass voice categories. Figure 5.2 gives the most commonly used voice classifications.

Other terms are applied to voices especially suitable for singing comic roles (such as *buffo* or *buffa*) or are assigned to various character roles. But those outlined above represent the standard terminology used to categorize most of the voice types recognized in Western vocal music.

Figure 5.2   *(Continued)*

FEMALE		MALE	
Medium Voice Range:	**Mezzo-soprano**	**Medium Voice Range:**	**Baritone**
Lyric mezzo-soprano	Light voice type with extensive lower range but limited top (not as high as soprano).	Lyric baritone	Light voice of medium range, between tenor and bass. Most common category of young male voices.
Dramatic mezzo-soprano	Very large, heavy, and usually dark quality in the mezzo range, usually capable of generous volume; similar in quality to contralto, but with slightly higher range.	Dramatic baritone	Heavy, dark voice, usually of generous power. More common among mature baritones.
Low Voice Range:	**Alto or Contralto**	**Low Voice Range:**	**Bass**
Contralto	Single category usually reserved for lowest, heaviest, and darkest female voices. About as uncommon in women as true bass among men.	Bass-baritone	As name implies, category combining bass and baritone qualities; usually has low range of bass and high range of baritone, thus unusually wide range.
		Basso cantante; basso cantabile	Lyric voice quality with low range; cantante is lighter in quality than cantabile.
		Basso profundo	Large, dark, bass voice, usually with very low range, at least to low C.
		Contrabass	Lowest of male voices, extending well below low C. Very rare.

Handwritten annotations: "Janet Baker", "Maureen Forrester", "Heinz Rehfuss singing Manuel", "Dietrich Fisher-Dieskau trained as a tenor"

Although it is important that you become aware of the many possibilities of voice classification, don't expect to categorize your own voice immediately. It is very difficult, and usually unwise, to categorize a young, untrained voice beyond the six basic ranges: soprano, mezzo-soprano, contralto, tenor, baritone, and bass. Even your range is uncertain at this stage of your development, and it may change substantially as you develop your vocal instrument. Many highly successful singers have changed voice categories even in midcareer: mezzos have become sopranos, baritones have become tenors, lyrics have become dramatics, etc. So don't be impatient to "fit into" a specific voice type. Let your voice develop naturally, in the direction that is correct for you. Remember that ultimately your voice is unique, anyway. Classifying voices is only a semantic convenience for use in discussing different voice types.

CLASSROOM EXERCISES

It is more difficult to treat the matter of registers in a group than most other vocal subjects, because each singer must be heard and worked with individually during all phases of instruction. Each voice behaves somewhat differently with regard to registers more than most other vocal factors. Therefore, while the exercises below may be introduced to the class together and practiced a few times as a group, each student must subsequently perform them alone. Only in this way can the instructor, the other class members, and the student know exactly how that particular voice is functioning. In the following exercises, no vowel is preferable to another. Use any suggested by your instructor.

For Exercise 5.1, begin on a note in the *lower* register, and without any interruption suddenly jump one octave higher, changing to upper register as you do so. Make an effort to minimize the change in quality as you change registers. Breathe only at the end of each phrase mark. This exercise is sung by both males and females on the same pitches.

Exercise 5.1   *Octave leaps through register change*

In Exercise 5.2, try to coordinate the change of registers so that it is as smooth and unnoticeable as possible. For both sexes the break will probably come around E above middle C in the first sequence, D in the next, D-sharp in the next, and so forth.

Exercise 5.2   *Arpeggios through the break*

Exercise 5.3 consists of major scales spanning two octaves. At first let your voice break wherever it seems to naturally. Then try to control the change, arbitrarily choosing a note on which to change. In this way you will become acquainted with the behavior of your voice's registers and be well on your way toward gaining coordination of them.

Exercise 5.3 *Two-octave scale through the break*

The scale in Exercise 5.4 consists of successive half-steps. Try to make the register change as *gradual* as possible. See if you can sustain the sensation of changing over two or three notes. If you succeed, you will have already begun to discover your "middle voice," or mixed register.

Exercise 5.4 *Chromatic scale through the break*

Exercise 5.5 is somewhat difficult and is best done individually. Both sexes begin on an E-flat above middle C. Use a pianissimo (very soft) tone in your *upper* register. Gradually crescendo (increase loudness) until your voice breaks into the lower register. At first the change will be abrupt and will probably feel quite awkward, but after a few tries you will gain some control. Continue the exercise on different nearby pitches, and begin to plan exactly at what point in the crescendo you want the change to take place. After you achieve some skill in *controlling* the change, try to sustain the point at which the change happens. Repeated attempts to do this will develop your "middle voice" coordination.

Exercise 5.5   *Single-tone crescendo-decrescendo through the break*

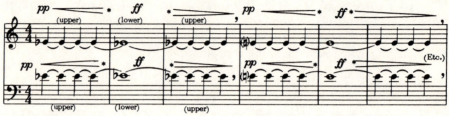

*Approximate point where the register change will take place.

ASSIGNMENTS

1. Add these exercises to your daily routine. Spend the most time on those that give you the most difficulty. Don't become discouraged if it seems you are not making quick progress. Coordination of the registers is one of the slowest vocal skills to develop.

2. Read Chapter 6.

3. Be prepared for your next song performance at the conclusion of Chapter 6.

6

ARTICULATION

SINGING WORDS

Singers are distinguished from other musicians in that their range of artistic expression includes a literary text. This extramusical expressive element can be communicated with musical success only if singers are capable of correct articulation of the words. *Singing* words, rather than speaking them, presents special articulative requirements. Singing a word usually alters the duration relationship between vowels and consonants in a spoken word. Vowels are sustained according to the rhythmic dictates of the music; consonants usually are not. Also, when words are sung, vowels are given specific pitch; most consonants are not. Thus the sung word is necessarily a distortion of the spoken one. However, if the sung word is well articulated, it will be as understandable as its spoken counterpart—and it can carry a musical expression that extends far beyond its literary meaning.

Everyday speech, particularly among Americans, tends to be quite imprecise, and varies with regional differences, accents, dialects, and the like, yet verbal communication is seldom a serious problem among people who speak the same language. When speech habits are carried into song, however, flaws are magnified. Impure vowel sounds and unclear consonants become unpleasantly evident, often rendering the song text unintelligible.

Conveying the words of a song clearly and expressively involves vocal skills beyond those required simply to produce beautiful tone. Yet correct articulation is an inseparable part of good tone production. Incorrect formation of vowels results in inferior tone quality. Faulty or careless production of consonants interferes with correct vowel formation. In short, poor articulation always results in poor singing.

The term *articulation* refers to the actions of the glottis, lips, tongue, teeth, hard palate, velum (soft palate), and jaws that combine to form word sounds. *Diction* is the precise formation and arrangement of these sounds into language patterns that accurately convey both the literary and the musical meaning of a song. If a song is sung with poor diction (faulty articulation of vowels and consonants), much more than the literary meaning is lost; the quality of the singing voice is also impaired, resulting in a musical loss.

Excellent singing diction can be achieved through the development of articulation skills. You can exert conscious control over the parts of your vocal apparatus that you use to articulate, as you can for breathing, phonation, resonance, and so forth. To gain control of these articulators, it is helpful to observe their anatomical structure and understand how they behave.

THE PHYSIOLOGY OF ARTICULATION

Figure 6.1 illustrates the organs of articulation. The articulation process usually requires the interaction of two or more of these articulators.

Probably the most important organ of articulation is the *tongue*, for it is needed to produce all vowels and many consonants. In articulating the words of commonly sung languages, the tongue comes into direct contact with every other articulator except the glottis. The position of the tongue, particularly in the back, shapes the vowel sounds and helps determine the consequent timbre of each. "Bright" vowels (*ee, ih, eh, à*) are formed by raising the back of the tongue; "dark" vowels (*ah, oh, oo*) are formed with lower tongue positions.

Consonants that are produced with the tongue are called *linguodental* when the tip of the tongue contacts the upper teeth (*th*is, *th*row, for example) and *linguoalveolar* when it touches the alveolar ridge just back of the upper teeth (*t, d, n, l, s, z*). When the top or sides of the tongue contact the hard palate, *linguopalatal* consonants result (*sh*ow, a*z*ure, *r*oll, *y*et). When the back of the tongue touches the soft palate (velum), *linguovelar* consonants are formed (*k, g, ng, x*).

The lips assist in the formation of vowel sounds, but are probably more important as articulators of consonants. *Bilabial* consonants are produced when the lips contact each other (*p, b, m, w*). *Labiodental* consonants result when the lower lip touches the upper teeth (*f, v*).

The *teeth*, *hard palate*, and *alveolar ridge*, all being stationary, function as articulators only in conjunction with the tongue. They are used primarily in the articulation of consonants.

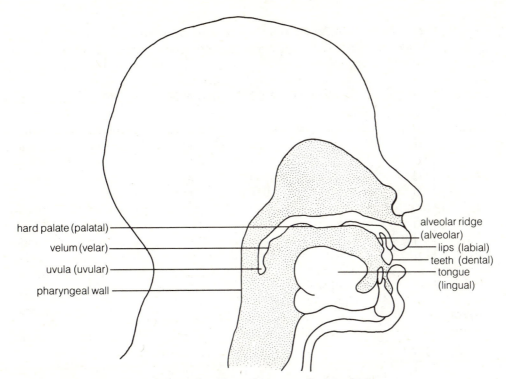

Figure 6.1   The articulators and points of articulation
The process of vocal articulation usually requires the interaction of two or more of the articulative organs.

The soft palate, or *velum,* is flexible, and its movement toward or away from the *pharyngeal wall* controls nasality in all vowel sounds. It is capable of closing off the nasal "door" altogether, eliminating nasal resonance. Action of the velum is necessary for the production of all nasal consonants (*m*an, ri*ng,* ca*ny*on).

While the glottis (the opening between the vocal folds) is primarily an organ of phonation, it functions as an articulator in both aspirated (*h*ow, *wh*en) and glottal (*oh, ah*) attacks. All vowel sounds and all *voiced* consonants (*b, d, g, j, l, m, n, r, v, z,* and combinations) originate at the glottis too.

THE INTERNATIONAL PHONETIC ALPHABET

In 1886 the International Phonetic Association standardized a system of symbols to represent all of the speech sounds of commonly spoken languages. These symbols, known as the International Phonetic Alphabet (IPA), constitute an invaluable tool for singers. Use of the IPA is an efficient way to analyze and systematize word sounds. This in turn is of great assistance in learning to articulate them correctly. The IPA also provides a word-sound "shorthand," making study of articulation more efficient.

The IPA is most useful when you memorize its symbols, but for the purposes of this course that is probably not necessary. We do need to use the symbols, however, to facilitate our study of articulation in this chapter. For that reason a list of the symbols is presented in Figure 6.2. This list of symbols identifies the vowel and consonant

Figure 6.2   The International Phonetic Alphabet

Common words in five languages are given as examples of the sound each symbol represents.

IPA symbol	English	Italian	German	French	Spanish
Vowels					
[i]	me	mi	liebe	qui	chico
[ɪ]	it	—	mit	—	—
[e]	chaotic	che	leben	chez	peso
[ɛ]	met	bello	besser	belle	usted
[æ]	cat	—	—	—	—
[a]	watch	—	—	ami	—
[ɑ]	father	casa	habe	—	pan
[ɒ]	hot (British)	—	—	—	—
[ɔ]	taught	cosa	Morgen	porte	ojo
[o]	obey	dove	wohl	beau	adobe
[ʊ]	book	—	Mutter	—	—
[u]	moon	luna	gut	mousse	mucho
[ʌ]	fun	—	—	—	—
[ə]	about	—	Liebe	je	—
[ɝ]	hurt	—	—	—	—
[ɚ]	after	—	—	—	—
[ø]	—	—	schön	peu	—
[œ]	—	—	können	coeur	—
[ʏ]	—	—	künste	—	—
[y]	—	—	über	lune	—
[ɛ̃]	—	—	—	fin	—
[ɑ̃]	—	—	—	ensemble	—
[õ]	—	—	—	ombre	—
[œ̃]	—	—	—	un	—
[j]	you	ieri	ja	hier	hoyo
[ɥ]	—	—	—	depuis	—
[w]	witch	uomo	—	oui	puerta
[ʎ]	lute	gli	—	fille	llamar
[ɑːɪ, aːi]	my	mai	mein	—	—
[ɔːɪ, ɔːi]	boy	poi	treu	—	—
[eːɪ, eːi,] [ɛːɪ, ɛːi]	say	sei	—	—	—
[oːʊ, oːu]	hoe	—	—	—	—
[ɑːʊ, ɑːu]	cow	causa	Haus	—	causa
[wɑːu]	wow	—	—	—	—
[joːu]	yo-yo	—	—	—	—

Row groups (left bracket labels): pure vowels, neutral vowels, mixed vowels, nasal vowels, glides, diphthongs and triphthongs.

Figure 6.2. *(Continued)*

IPA symbol	English	Italian	German	French	Spanish
			Consonants		
[b]	box	bene	Bahn	bien	bueno
[ç]	—	—	ich	—	—
[d]	do	dente	des	du	duerme
[dʒ]	joy	gioia	—	—	—
[dz]	adds	azzura	—	—	—
[f]	fine	forte	fast	fort	fuerte
[g]	go	gondola	gabe	grande	guerra
[gs]	exile	—	—	exil	—
[h]	high	—	hoch	—	jugar
[k]	kick	caro	kalt	que	cantar
[ʒ]	measure	—	—	jour	—
[ʒd]	edged	—	—	—	—
[ks]	lax	—	Luchs	luxe	excavar
[l]	long	lungo	legen	les	lado
[ɫ]	milk	—	—	—	—
[m]	man	mamma	Mutter	mon	madre
[n]	no	naso	nein	non	andar
[ŋ]	ring	uengo	Finger	—	banca
[ɲ]	onion	ognuno	—	agneau	señor
[p]	pan	padre	passen	pas	padre
[r]	red	rosso	reiten	rouge	rojo
[s]	sing	sangue	essen	sang	si
[ʃ]	show	sciocco	schon	chaud	—
[ʃt]	rushed	—	standen	—	—
[t]	two	tutto	tal	tout	todo
[ts]	rats	zio	Zimmer	—	—
[tʃ]	church	cielo	klatsch	—	charro
[v]	very	verde	warm	vous	verde
[x]	—	—	ach	—	jabon
[hw]	when	—	—	—	—
[z]	zebra	casa	Sohn	zele	isla
[θ]	thing	—	—	—	cinco
[ð]	there	—	—	—	lado
[ʔ]	(Glottal plosive that occurs in all languages, dependent upon the inflection and stress. An example occurs in the exclamation oh-oh!)				

sounds of the five languages most frequently sung in this country. Although most of the songs used in this course will be in English, symbols for the other languages are included for comparison and to enhance the value of the list as a reference tool. Frequent reference to this list can greatly benefit your acquisition of articulation skills.

VOWELS

Vowels are the parts of sung words that carry the vocal tone. Consonants interrupt or partially obstruct the tone in order to create words. Both are essential to singing, as they are to speech. Without vowels there would be no vehicle for the melody; without consonants a song would have no words. Vowels usually receive more attention from singers than consonants, because the manner of their formation largely determines the beauty of the vocal tone. Also much more time is spent on vowels in singing than on consonants. Clear, pure vowels are usually considered the basis of good tone production.

Vowels may be classified in three main categories: *tongue* vowels, *lip* vowels, and *mixed* vowels. As the terms suggest, tongue vowels are formed primarily by the position of the tongue, lip vowels require more involvement of the lips, and mixed vowels are formed by mixing a tongue vowel with a lip vowel. Figure 6.3, when used with reference to the IPA, clearly shows these relationships.

As the IPA examples in Figure 6.2 illustrate, none of the mixed vowels occurs in English; they are included in Figure 6.3 to show the relationships among common vowel sounds. Figure 6.3 also does not show the *neutral* vowels (ə, ʌ, ɝ, ɚ), which require little involvement of either lips or tongue.

To experiment with the vowel series shown in Figure 6.3, position yourself in front of a mirror and sing or speak each vowel while observing your tongue and lips. Go through the tongue vowels from the lowest tongue position, [a], to the highest, [i], and then reverse the order. Note that it is primarily the *back* of the tongue that rises and lowers. Now use the same procedure with the lip vowels, observing the gradual change from an open, relaxed position in [a] to a pursed, rounded one in [u]. To produce the mixed vowels (not used in English), simply shape the lips for the symbol in the right column and sing or speak the vowel sound on the same line in the left column. The resultant vowel sound will be that indicated by the symbol between the two.

Also belonging to the vowel category are the vowel combinations of *diphthongs* and *triphthongs*. As the names suggest, a diphthong is a combination of two vowels

	tongue vowels		mixed vowels		lip vowels	
high	i	———	y	———	u	rounded
↑	e		ø		o	↑
tongue	ɪ	———	Y	———	ʊ	**lips**
↓	ɛ	———	œ	———	ɔ	↓
	æ				ɒ	
low	a	———		———	a	open

Figure 6.3   Classes of vowels
Tongue vowels are distinguished from one another by the high or low position of the tongue; lip vowels by the rounded or open position of the lips.

and a triphthong, three. These vowel combinations are sounded within a single syllable. The English language has many diphthongs and a good number of triphthongs. Common diphthongs are [a:i] (m<u>i</u>ne), [a:U] (n<u>ow</u>), [ɛ:i] (d<u>ay</u>), [o:u] (gr<u>ow</u>), [ɔ:i] (b<u>oy</u>), and [i:u] (y<u>ou</u>). Examples of triphthongs are [u:a:i] (w<u>i</u>se), [jo:u] (<u>yo-yo</u>), [u:o:u] (w<u>oe</u>), [i:E:i] (<u>yea</u>), and [u:a:u] (<u>wow</u>).

In articulating diphthongs and triphthongs the singer must take care to treat the primary vowel as a vowel and the secondary one(s) as consonant(s). In most English diphthongs, the primary vowel is the *first* one and in triphthongs it is the *middle* one. Only the primary vowel may be sustained in singing; although secondary ones may carry pitch, they must be treated as voiced consonants and must not be sustained.

Purity of vowels is one of the most important concerns of the singer. An ill-formed vowel will not resonate well, and much of the beauty of tone will be lost. In addition, the sound of the word in which the vowel occurs will be distorted. Most successful voice teachers recommend that their students vocalize the common vowels daily to achieve vowel purity. Correct vowel production cannot be taught successfully from any book. The sounds must be *heard;* then they must be imitated. A teacher with a keen ear must listen to the student's efforts and suggest the adjustments needed to correct faulty production. For example, an [u] vowel may be attempted with the lips too rounded, resulting in a muffled, dull quality. The teacher must be able to identify this fault to correct it. Students in a class have the advantage of seeing and hearing others undergo this process, which is an invaluable learning experience.

Perhaps the most common error untrained singers make in producing vowels is to depend too much upon the *mouth* to form the sound and too little on the *back of the tongue.* The result is production of vowels that do not match one another in color and quality. Watching in a mirror and deliberately avoiding unnecessary mouth movement will usually bring immediate improvement in vowel purity and consistency. A helpful psychological image to keep in mind is: Form the vowels in the pharynx, not in the mouth. (Remember that the front wall of the oropharynx *is* the back of the tongue.) The result will be clear, well-formed vowels, and a rich, resonant tone quality that is consistent from vowel to vowel.

CONSONANTS

While vowels are the *carriers* of vocal tone, consonants are the *interruptors* of it. In singing, as in speech, the interruption of vowel sound is necessary for the intelligible production of words. In 1894 Manuel Garcia, one of the most famous teachers of singing in his day (and the inventor of the laryngoscope, an instrument for observing the interior of the larynx), wrote:

> Consonants are the skeletons of words. Applied to song, they have three distinct functions:
>
> 1. To convey the sense of words
> 2. To beat time and mark the rhythm by their percussions
> 3. Through their varied degrees of energy [to] declare the state of activity of the sentiment, just as vowels manifest its nature.[1]

---

1. Quoted in Brent Jeffrey Monahan, *The Art of Singing* (Metuchen, N.J., and London: Scarecrow Press, 1978), pp. 191–92.

nant at the beginning of the next word, special care must be taken. In everyday speech most Americans are quite careless in these circumstances. "Sweet charm" [swit tʃarm], for example, would usually be spoken as [switʃarm]. In speech the phrase is not difficult to understand, but when sung it can easily sound like "sweech arm" if not articulated carefully.

Glottal stops [ʔ] are often dropped in everyday speech, usually without rendering words unintelligible. However, when sung, the same phrases can take on entirely new, and often unfortunate, meanings: "When I'm old" becomes "When I mould" if no glottal stroke is articulated before the o. Dropping the glottal stroke before the e in "Upon our ears" will produce "upon our rears," when the phrase is sung.

A final consideration in good diction is to avoid anticipating voiced consonants. When a singer articulates a voiced consonant too early, the result is a double misfortune: (1) part of the time value of the preceding vowel is stolen; and (2) the voiced consonant is sustained, to fill the time that belonged to the vowel. As mentioned before, sustained voiced consonants are unpleasant and unnecessarily distort words in singing. They are appropriate only in country and western music.

To experiment with this aspect of diction, sing the following two phrases on a single pitch, holding each word for two beats: "Come and see" and "Will she tell?" To see how consonant anticipation sounds, the first time go immediately to the voiced consonant and then sustain that consonant until the two beats are completed: "Commmm annnnd seeeee"; "Willll sheee tellll?" Notice how unpleasant this execution sounds. Now sing it correctly, with long vowels and short consonants. Notice the difference: "Cooooome aaaaand seeeee"; "Wiiiill sheeee teeeell?"

Make special note of this concept, for it is one of the singer's most important means of achieving excellent diction. The melody can be carried with great success and with vocal beauty by the long, uninterrupted vowels; the words are clearly discernible due to the short, clean consonants. Think of this approach each time you learn a new song. Soon it will become a valuable habit.

CLASSROOM EXERCISES

Surely the most effective way to practice articulation skills is by applying the techniques of good diction to actual song literature. In the early stages of learning these techniques, however, it is helpful to isolate words, syllables, and even particular vowels and consonants, in order to understand their proper production thoroughly. The following exercises may be practiced first by the class as a group. Then each student should execute them alone so that the instructor can listen carefully for vowel purity, clean consonant articulation, correct liaison, and the like. Certain devices should be incorporated into your daily practice routine, at least until you have thoroughly mastered them.

Isolation of the five basic vowel sounds in Exercise 6.1 will give a clear indication of how you now perceive and produce each—the position taken by the tongue, lips, jaw, and so forth. The vowels should be sung alone first, then used in a word. Suggested words are given in the list below. The class should concentrate on each vowel, first as a group, then individually, before moving to the next one.

Exercise 6.1 *Pure vowels on five-note scales*

[i]	be___	free___	plea___se
[e]	may___	ta___ke	rai___se
[ɑ]	ah___	da___rk	wa___s
[o]	oh___	gho___st	jo___ke
[u]	too___	lo___se	loo___m

Consistency of vowel color is desirable, because it allows a voice to sound balanced and even. Radical changes in the position of the tongue, lips, and jaw when moving from one vowel to another will usually result in unpleasant and unnecessary changes in vowel color. In Exercise 6.2, keep all parts of your mouth and jaw as relaxed as possible, and try to avoid excessive movement when shifting from one vowel to the next.

Exercise 6.2 *Legato vowel change on sustained pitch*

Exercises 6.3–6.6 develop articulative flexibility for consonants. They are musical "tongue twisters" that promote agility of the organs of articulation, particularly the tongue and lips. Gradually increase the speed of each exercise.

Exercise 6.3   *Repeated ascending triplets with text*

Bring back the boy's big bright blue base - ball bats

Bring back the boy's big bright blue base - ball bats

Bring back the boy's big bright blue base - ball bats (Etc.)

Exercise 6.4   *Repeated up and down triplets with text*

Waf-fles are won-der-ful but they will wid-en your waist;

Waf-fles are won-der-ful but they will wid-en your waist   (Etc.)

Exercise 6.5 *Ascending and descending duplets with text*

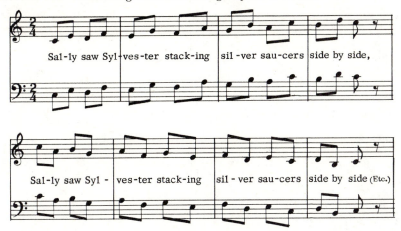

Raise entire sequence by half-steps.

Exercise 6.6 *Arpeggios with text*

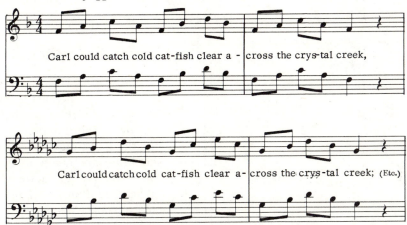

Finally, to practice connecting words, sing one of the following songs while applying all the principles of singing diction you have learned in this chapter:

1. *Willow Song*, pages 148–151.

2. *From Far, from Eve and Morning*, pages 127–128.

ASSIGNMENTS

1. Incorporate the Classroom Exercises, particularly those devoted to vowel purity and consonant agility, into your daily practice routine.

2. Be prepared to perform your next song for the class in the next session.

7

COORDINATION

VOCAL TECHNIQUE

Virtually every vocal skill you have acquired over the past few weeks has been a result of developing or improving coordination. Your breathing technique, for example, should now be much improved because you have greater coordination in your breathing mechanism than before; your articulation skills are probably greater because your articulation mechanisms are now better coordinated; and so forth. The main objective of this chapter is to help you begin to combine these singing skills (some still largely undeveloped) into a single, coordinated vocal technique. This process will not be completed quickly, certainly not within the duration of this course. It will take many months, probably several years, before you begin to feel secure in your total singing technique. Even then you will undoubtedly develop further if you continue to work. However, in the meantime, you can thoroughly enjoy using your singing voice while it is developing. If your skills are exceptional, you may even engage in considerable public performance during this development process.

It is important to note that all the essential elements of singing are interrelated. Developing excellent resonating ability is significantly dependent upon good breathing technique; articulative skills are valuable only if tone production is good; and so on. The early stages of training isolate different elements to develop one skill at a time. But none of the separate skills can be *fully* developed until all are integrated into a coordinated singing technique. This technique then becomes an entity greater than the sum of its parts.

MUSCULAR INTERFERENCE

To achieve a coordinated vocal technique, you must identify and eliminate problems that can limit its potential. Surely the most common of these is muscular interference, usually referred to simply as *tension*. Muscular interference is the intrusion of muscles not required for singing into that process. The result is an obstruction of the activity of muscles required for the singing process, which either reduces or destroys their effectiveness. Muscular interference is a common concern of singers because its potential sources are so numerous. In fact, nearly every singer is at some time plagued by it, in one form or another. Indeed, for some it can be a serious vocal problem that causes considerable singing difficulties. The most common areas in which muscular interference can take place include the tongue, the extrinsic muscles of the larynx, the muscles of the jaw and neck, and the abdominal muscles.

The *tongue* is often referred to as the most "unruly" part of the singing mechanism. This is largely because, although it is a very active component of the singing apparatus, much of its activity is at first below the level of consciousness—it seems to have a mind of its own. If you have ever looked into a mirror and tried to hold your tongue perfectly still, or if you have tried to make it assume and hold a specific shape, you well understand the point. Yet the tongue can easily make the most complex of movements and shapes in the production of speech and singing. To gain conscious control of these movements you must first of all achieve freedom from muscular interference.

Eight muscles control the movements of the tongue that are primarily used in speech and singing. Four of these are *intrinsic* (inside) and four are *extrinsic* (outside). The actions of the intrinsic muscles in general move different parts of the tongue (for example, raising the tip only or "curling" the sides), while the extrinsic muscles tend to move the entire tongue, up, down, back, and forward. One common form of muscular interference in the tongue is general tension in the intrinsic muscles, which causes the tongue to become too rigid to freely assume the correct positions for pure vowel sounds. The result is inconsistent tone color among vowels and, frequently, pitch discrepancies (see the discussion of intonation, later in this chapter). Tension in certain extrinsic muscles is also common. This pulls the tongue too far backward and downward, producing a covered or dark tone quality and usually vocal fatigue.

Removing muscular interference is seldom easy, because it involves learning to *disengage* certain muscles, rather than simply to engage others. It is usually achieved through conscious relaxation. Sometimes a particular exercise helps. The following one will go far to free tension of the tongue muscles and allow the necessary conscious relaxation to take place.[1] With the tip of your tongue low in the mouth and the back of your tongue high (as it is in forming the [i] vowel), move your entire tongue rapidly back and forth in the mouth: forward, back, forward, back, forward, back. You may need to start slowly and gradually work up to a faster oscillation. When the movement becomes free and you can accomplish it with ease, add vowel sounds, starting with [i], while continuing the tongue motion. Then, one by one, move to the lower tongue vowels: [I] [e], [E], [ae], [a], [o], [u]. Keep the tongue movement as free and relaxed as possible. This exercise should be practiced several minutes daily until any rigidity in the tongue muscles eases.

The *extrinsic muscles of the larynx* are among the most troublesome causes of interference in the singing process, because they are used in swallowing, which moves the entire larynx substantially. When the larynx is out of its normal, relaxed and low position, the singing process is seriously disturbed. You will recall from Chapter 3 that when you swallow, the larynx rises to meet the hyoid bone, and singing is impossible. If these muscles are only slightly contracted and the larynx moves up only partway, singing is possible but is much more difficult than usual; in fact it can be done only with substantial vocal strain. Unfortunately, in young, untrained voices (and in poorly trained ones) this is often exactly what happens. Although the swallowing muscles are under some conscious control, they tend to engage involuntarily during the singing process. This is most likely to happen when singers attempt the highest pitches. Then the muscles become interfering muscles that directly impede the singing process. Singers must learn to keep these muscles disengaged, or relaxed, at all times during singing. The simplest way for you to learn to do this is to become conscious of the position of your larynx and endeavor to keep it in its normal, unraised position while singing. This is best done by observing your larynx in a mirror while you are vocalizing. It may also be accomplished by placing a finger lightly against the tip of your larynx to feel for any motion. (Don't try to hold your larynx down with your finger, however. Conscious relaxation is the only successful method.)

Another potentially offending muscle closely related to the larynx is the *mylo-hyoid*, which runs from the chin to the hyoid bone. You can feel it if you place your thumb in the depression just below and behind your chin. While holding your thumb here, swallow. What do you feel? The depression disappears, and the muscle contracts against your thumb (at the same time the larynx rises). This contraction is part of the swallowing process, like that of the other extrinsic muscles of the larynx, and similarly can impair free vocal production. But, unlike the other muscles, this one is easy to check for tension from time to time while vocalizing. If it is not relaxed (soft to the touch of your thumb), your singing and your voice will suffer.

Muscular interference of the *jaw and neck* muscles can cause serious disturbances in tone production and undue vocal fatigue. In fact a tense or tight jaw can make it impossible to practice or perfect the tongue exercise described above—an example of the interaction of various muscular interferences. Tension in the neck or jaw is often so pronounced it is clearly visible. Its effect on tone production usually is a tense, strident quality. The voice also tires quickly and may become hoarse.

Jaw and neck tension often cannot be removed abruptly. Relaxation exercises

---

1. I am indebted to Joseph Klein, author of *Singing Technique* (Princeton, N.J.: D. Van Nostrand, 1967), for demonstrating this exercise at one of his highly informative vocal workshops.

help a great deal. One of these is to roll your head slowly about in a circular manner while humming a simple vocalise (a simple five-note ascending and descending scale, for example). Be sure your teeth are not clenched. Now, continuing to roll your head, drop your jaw and open your mouth to a vowel sound. Continue this, changing vowels from time to time, and concentrate on relaxing your neck and jaw muscles. Another helpful device specifically for jaw tension is to place two or three fingers, held together vertically, between your teeth while vocalizing. Jaw tension will cause you to bite down on your fingers (making you acutely aware of the tension). It is also useful to watch your jaw and neck in the mirror while you practice. Look for tense muscles, and consciously relax them. Then concentrate on the sensations you feel when these muscles are relaxed. Memorize these sensations so you can recreate them at will.

Even the *abdominal muscles* can act as interfering muscles, if they do not relax during inhalation. When they are tense they can restrict the downward movement of the diaphragm and cause your breathing to be shallow. Tense abdominal muscles are a very common result of nervousness during performance. What happens is a vicious cycle: the tense muscles restrict breathing, which results in inadequate breath for singing; this causes anxiety, which results in more tension; and so forth. The most effective way to avoid tension in the abdominal muscles is to take several deep breaths before beginning to sing and to develop a habit of consciously relaxing these muscles when inhaling. A psychological image that may be helpful is: When you inhale, just let your belly drop.

These are but the most common sources of muscular interference. Certain singers experience other forms. If you feel undue vocal stress, hoarseness, or other physical discomfort while or after singing, you may be virtually assured that muscular interference is present. To become a skilled singer, you must first locate it and then eliminate it.

INTONATION

Just as the essential elements of good singing are interrelated, so are many of the vocal problems that can impede its development. Poor intonation (singing out of tune or "off key") is very often the result of some form of tension, or muscular interference. It is rare indeed that sharp tones (*above* the correct pitch) or flat ones (*below* the correct pitch) are caused by a "poor ear," unless the singer is simply being careless or not concentrating. Oddly, tension causes sharp tones in some singers and flat tones in others. It is not always possible to determine if the same *kinds* of tension produce these opposite conditions. But in either case elimination of the tension nearly always improves intonation.

As mentioned earlier, tension in the tongue can cause impure and uneven vowel sounds. The pitch of an improperly formed vowel can sound true to you (since you hear most of the tone from the *inside*, or through the inner ear) when it is really badly out of tune. Doing the tongue exercise suggested above, and concentrating upon vowel purity (with the assistance of a listener with a keen ear) in practicing vocalises, will help you eliminate tongue tension and improve any intonation difficulties caused by faulty vowel production.

Another common contributor to poor intonation in some singers is incorrect *resonation* (you may wish to review Chapter 4). When the resonators (laryngopharynx, oropharynx, and nasopharynx) do not adjust to match the pitch produced by the vibrator (vocal cords), faulty pitch (as well as poor tone quality) results. This is true not only for the human voice but also for other instruments. For example if a trumpet player adjusts the tension of his or her lips (the vibrator) to play a C but depresses the first and third valves—the fingering for D—the result will be a pitch that is neither C nor D and a tone that is weak and ill focused. In the voice, the resonators are adjusted almost unconsciously (there are no keys to press) and largely "by ear." If the resonator system is obstructed in any way—for example, if the laryngopharynx is constricted (tight throat), if the tongue obstructs the oropharynx, or if the soft palate closes off the nasopharynx—the system cannot respond correctly to the pitches produced by the vocal cords. Poor intonation and poor tone production result. This is a highly complex problem and requires the attention of a skilled voice teacher. If you have intonation difficulties and incorrect resonance seems to be the cause, your instructor may be able to help you privately or recommend a teacher for you.

There are more general physical causes for occasional pitch problems, and their remedies are obvious. Fatigue, inadequate breath technique, and attempting to sing too softly to control pitch accurately are among the most common physical causes for flat singing. Sharp singing often results from extreme nervousness or anxiety and from attempts to sing too loudly, forcing the voice.

Good intonation is a prized virtue among all singers, for without it the finest vocal quality is of little value. For many singers it is a gift, a quality that does not demand work. But, even if you experience some difficulty at first, it is attainable if you have the patience and perseverance to eliminate the problems that can obstruct it.

EXTENDING PITCH AND DYNAMIC RANGES

Even a voice of modest beauty can be impressive and can convey a great deal of expression if it is capable of a pitch range from very high notes to very low ones, and a dynamic compass from very loud to very soft. In untrained voices both pitch and dynamic ranges are usually limited, but as vocal skills develop both tend to increase naturally. Certain steps can be taken to hasten this progress, but as a beginning singer you should avoid viewing range and dynamic extension as separate and immediate goals. Although they both can be objects of concentrated attention, they are interrelated with other essential elements of singing and depend on them for successful development. Probably the most important of these is efficient breath management. If either the supply of breath or the breath support technique is inadequate, attempts to extend range and dynamics will be severely limited. This subject is deliberately placed well into our course of study in the expectation that by now you will have adequately developed the basic techniques of breathing and tone production to allow the pursuit of extended ranges.

Possibly the most basic concept in extending your pitch range is that the higher you sing the more breath *energy* is required, and the lower you descend the less is needed; the breath *support*, however, must remain constant at all times. Efforts to force more and more air through the vocal folds to reach the lowest tones will not succeed. Using less than adequate breath on the highest pitches will cause tension and result in a pinched tone, as well as considerable discomfort. One helpful concept for extending your range while maintaining excellent vocal quality is to think of "thinning" vocal cords as you ascend and "thickening" cords as you descend. In other words, think of a lighter voice quality up high and a heavier one down low.

More than likely, over a period of time, you will find that you can extend the upper limit of your singing range more than the lower one. This is because the lower extreme of your voice is more or less predetermined genetically. You cannot sing lower than the length and thickness of your vocal cords will allow; you can't learn to make them appreciably longer and thicker. The upper limit of your voice range, however, depends more on skill and coordination. Most untrained voices are capable of significant range extension at the top with adequate study and training. Three additional suggestions may help you extend your upper voice:

1. Particularly in the early stages of development, do not attempt to sing high tones too softly—don't inhibit the tone. Use plenty of breath and support.

2. Opening your mouth wider for the highest pitches may make them easier to produce. This seems to vary among individuals. Experimentation will determine if it is helpful for you.

3. Think of your highest tones as more *nasally resonant* than lower ones. Although this technique is rejected by some teachers and singers, those who try it usually find it very helpful. Slightly nasalizing vowels helps keep the soft palate from closing, and thereby gives you the maximum benefit of the resonators that match the highest pitches and their overtones. Not only will you find the highest tones easier to produce, but they will also sound more beautiful. A word of caution: this technique must be learned with the assistance of a teacher *with a keen ear*. You will not be able to hear the precise timbre of your own tone accurately, at least at first. If you overnasalize, the tone may become unpleasantly *nasal*. The desired result is a tone that is nasally *resonant*—that is, rich with high overtones.

Changes in dynamics account for much of the expressive potential of any musical instrument. A thundering *fortissimo* (very loud) and a barely audible *pianissimo* (very soft) are equally compelling. In the mature, highly trained voice the contrast can be quite awesome. Achieving such a range of dynamics requires great control and coordination, skills not often attained quickly. You can begin extending your dynamic range immediately, however, by applying a few basic principles. In the early stages of dynamic range extension, practice in the most comfortable part of your pitch range, not in the high or low extremes. Be sure your breathing technique is adequate; dynamic changes require excellent control of the breath support system. Singing softly requires even more sophisticated breath control than loud singing, as the diaphragm must resist the abdominal muscles more strongly. Many singers find it easier to produce their softest tones by thinking about a very light quality with a bright, forward focus and imagining the sensation of a *hum* in their tone. The concept of humming is equally helpful in producing powerful but pleasing loud tones. However, at louder levels the quality is often imagined as somewhat heavier, especially in the middle and lower ranges. Successful loud production is the result of a combination of well-controlled breath energy and sophisticated management of the resonance system. If the resonance system functions efficiently, loud singing can be virtually effortless—and beautiful. Possibly the most helpful concept in developing more volume in your tone is to imagine and feel a great deal of *space* in all of your resonators. Sense an open throat, a free, humming sensation in the nasal cavities, an adequate space in the mouth and in back of the tongue. Never drive the voice; achieve your loudest singing through generous *size* of the tone, not by brute force. Specific exercises for extending both pitch ranges and dynamic levels are given at the end of this chapter.

VIBRATO

Even to the most musically unsophisticated ear, the vibrato in a vocal tone is one of its most distinctive characteristics. Listeners who don't know what vibrato is and aren't aware they are hearing it nonetheless respond to its existence (or lack) in a given voice probably more than to any other single quality. Vibrato occurs naturally in every physically normal, free, and well-coordinated human voice. It is a normal condition resulting from nerve impulses activating muscles as they do, not constantly but in pulses. When vibrato is not present, either conscious inhibition ("straight-tone" singing), or some form of muscular interference (tension) is preventing it.

Normal vibrato in the human voice is a more or less regular, synchronized, fluctuation of pitch, intensity, and timbre. The frequency of its pulsations is optimally between six and eight per second. If the vibrato rate is slower than this, it is perceived by most listeners as an annoying "wobble" (often a characteristic of very heavy, dark voices, particularly among older singers). A faster rate is heard by most people as an irritating bleat; in fact, the Italians refer to such a vibrato as *voce di capra* (goat voice), which has been translated by some American singers as "a goat in the throat." Untrained voices may have little or no vibrato, simply because the singing mechanism is not yet coordinated, and muscular tension in one form or another is preventing the voice from functioning with complete freedom.

Although vibrato occurs naturally and unconsciously in the well-coordinated voice, skilled singers still have considerable control over it. They can increase or decrease both its speed and its intensity. A common example used by many contemporary popular entertainers is the device of starting a sustained note at the end of a phrase more or less "straight" (without vibrato) and then releasing the vibrato midway through its duration and for the remainder of the tone. Concert and opera singers can consciously control their vibrato to serve their needs in coloratura singing (florid passages of music requiring great speed and agility). The speed of the vibrato is coordinated with the speed of the notes so that the peak of each vibrato pulse articulates the individual note. The result is often a technical display of speed, precision, and accuracy comparable with that of any manufactured musical instrument.

While the presence of vibrato depends on the coordination of other basic elements of vocal technique, its development can be encouraged by specific exercises. Because the muscle and nerve impulses related to the breathing mechanism seem to affect the vibrato more than those originating elsewhere (in the larynx, for example), a free and coordinated breathing technique is probably the most crucial prerequisite. The pulsation exercise presented in Chapter 2 is valuable for encouraging natural vibrato. In fact, if you have mastered this exercise and it is free and easy for you, your vibrato is probably already apparent and developing well. If not, give special attention to the exercise; it will yield positive results. Some voice teachers also advocate a consciously induced fluctuation of pitch, but this has not proved helpful to many beginning students. Experimentation will tell you if it is of benefit to you.

Remember that vibrato is an integral part of your coordinated vocal technique and accounts for a large percentage of the potential beauty of your voice. It is perhaps the most unique and deeply personal quality of your voice. A well-developed vibrato will reflect your feelings and emotions with great accuracy, enhancing the expressive powers of your singing.

LEGATO TECHNIQUE

When applied to music, the Italian word *legato* means to produce successive tones in a smooth, even, connected, and continuous style. This would be easier for singers if they did not sing with words. Words, particularly those with beginning and ending consonants, tend to separate vocal tones and interfere with a legato style, as mentioned in Chapter 6. Consequently, singing tones can be unconnected unless some special attention is given to developing legato technique. The great majority of vocal music, both serious and light, is written to be performed in legato style. The sustained, connected nature of this style is ideally suited for singing expressively and for exposing the beauty of the voice. For that reason it is an essential technique for every singer. The expressive flow of a song, known to musicians as *phrasing*, cannot be achieved without it.

Legato technique requires coordination skills. Its success depends largely on knowing precisely when to conclude one note and initiate another, and how to connect the two in a way that does not disturb the flow of the musical line. How do you develop such skills? One of the swiftest ways is to learn to execute an articulative device in music known as the *slur*. The slur connects notes of different pitches without interruption. Slurs are accomplished by quickly moving from one note to the next *while* the sound is being produced. In instruments of infinite pitch (the bowed strings, the trombone, the voice, and so on) the infinity of pitches *between* the two notes in question are actully sounded, but so quickly that the ear responds only to the first and last pitches. All the pitches between are heard as part of a very smooth connection. Try the following slur exercise: Sing C (middle C for women, an octave lower for men) and, without stopping the tone, move quickly and smoothly to the G above. Then, again without stopping the tone, move back to the C in a similar manner. *The movement must be quick and smooth, and without accents on any of the pitches.* Now sing a five-note ascending and descending scale from C up to G and back down to C, moving smoothly from note to note without interruption or stress on any particular pitch. This technique should be used consistently in legato singing, particularly when phrases are indicated by long, curved lines (♪♩ ♩ ♪♩ ♩♪) and when the slur notation, a short curved line (♩♪) connects two or three notes. The slur is not to be confused with the *portamento* (glide or slide), which is done more slowly, so that the infinity of pitches between the written notes *is* heard; if a slur is done too slowly, it is perceived as an offensive smear, or *glissando*. Glissandos are used only for specific emotional or comical effects when specified by the composer.

Excellent legato singing depends on two requirements that are really one: that each note be sustained as long as possible before moving to the next note, and that all vowels be held as long as possible while consonants are given as short a duration as possible (as described in Chapter 6). The benefits of this method of achieving a smooth legato are twofold: the vocal line is uninterrupted, and the words are clearly intelligible.

Sing the first verse of "Breake Now My Heart" (pp. 121–122 of the Song Anthology) giving special attention to legato style. After a reasonable amount of practice, tape-record your efforts (or have a class member listen to you). Is your vocal line connected and seamless? Or do you hear small hesitations and changes from one note to the next that are not smooth? Do you anticipate consonants, particularly voiced ones, "cheating" the vowels? Are there smears between notes of different pitches? If your recorded effort still has a few of these flaws, spend some more time on the excerpt, giving special attention to the particular problems, and record your singing again. Remember that legato singing is a skill; skills are achieved and perfected through practice.

FLEXIBILITY AND AGILITY

If you have ever heard a coloratura soprano speeding brilliantly through a difficult aria replete with intricate, florid ornamentation, trills, and other embellishments, you no doubt marveled that the human voice is capable of such velocity and precision. The quality that enables such pyrotechnical displays is called vocal *agility*. A voice is capable of such agility only if it is sufficiently *flexible*, that is, able to make adjustments of pitch, timbre, intensity, and so forth, with great speed and accuracy. A voice may be beautiful without being particularly agile, and it can still sing an abundance of literature quite successfully—indeed, the vast majority of vocal music (particularly in the popular field) makes few or no demands for agility. However, vocal technique is incomplete without the development of flexibility; it is needed for a voice to develop its complete range of technical expressiveness. Moreover, in training the voice to become more flexible, many additional benefits are realized: muscular interference is reduced, allowing greater vocal freedom; a lighter approach usually results in the upper part of the voice, often extending the high range; adjustments of pitch, tone quality, and dynamics become easier to make more quickly and with greater accuracy; legato singing improves due to greater control; and finally, the potential for vocal agility is established.

How do you train your voice to become more flexible? It is done most successfully with what is known as *velocity* exercises. Just as runners cannot learn to run fast by practicing running slowly, neither can singers make their voices more flexible and agile by practicing only slow, sustained vocalises. Velocity exercises are designed to help "move" the voice—to teach it to respond to musical requirements with speed, precision, and grace. The exercises may seem difficult at first, and you probably won't master them overnight. But, if you approach them positively, deliberately, and *slowly at first*, they will prove remarkably effective. Exercises for developing flexibility are generally omitted from beginning voice texts, probably on the premise that they are too advanced for the untrained voice. However, experience has proved that it is much easier to maintain the natural flexibility of youthful voices with such exercises than it is to retrain voices after they have become more or less set in a technique that excludes flexibility.

Vocalises for developing flexibility and agility are included in the Classroom

Exercises that follow. They are somewhat more complex than most prior vocalises, and their proper execution should be demonstrated by your instructor. They are the final exercises to be presented in this course, and you will probably not master them until well after the course is completed. Continue to make use of them as long as you continue to sing. You will not only increase the flexibility of your voice but contribute significantly to the improvement of your complete singing technique.

CLASSROOM EXERCISES

Specific exercises are given for each coordination consideration treated in this chapter. Once the exercises have been introduced and practiced in class, you may find it helpful to review the topics as you pursue the exercises alone. Mastery of some of the more difficult vocalises may take considerable time; do not be discouraged if you are not able to sing them perfectly at first. Remember that you are working to develop your vocal coordination. Mastery of the exercises, followed by continued practice of them, will help you achieve the skills required for a dependable, coordinated vocal technique.

Exercises 7.1 and 7.2 are intended to help eliminate *muscular interference*. Review the exercises suggested in the discussion of this problem earlier before adding the vocalises. Using the technique of the tongue exercise described, and holding your jaw relaxed, vocalize Exercise 7.1. The bulk of your tongue should move freely forward and back with each successive [j]. Practice this vocalise with all vowels.

Exercise 7.1   *Ascending and descending five-note scales*

Continue to as high a note as comfortable, then repeat with other vowels and gradually increase tempo.

Observing your larynx in a mirror, or touching it lightly with your fingertips, sing Exercise 7.2, consciously relaxing all nonsinging muscles of the larynx so that it does not move up and down. Use all vowels.

Exercise 7.2 *Legato octaves*

Continue to as high a note as comfortable, then repeat with other vowels.

Chromatic (half-step) scales are among the most helpful devices to sharpen your awareness of *intonation*. Sing Exercise 7.3 first with the piano, then alone. Check your pitch at the end of each scale (ascending and descending).

Exercise 7.3 *Chromatic scales*

Continue to as high a note as comfortable, then repeat with other vowels.

Exercises 7.4 and 7.5 work on *extending your high range*. Remember to think of your tone production as high, light, slightly nasal, and forward. In Exercise 7.4, put a slight accent on the first note of each descending arpeggio.

Exercise 7.4 *Descending arpeggios*

Continue to as high a note as comfortable, then repeat with other vowels.

In Exercise 7.5, notice especially the crescendo on the highest note of each scale. Use all vowels, emphasizing [e] and [u].

Exercise 7.5   *Ascending and descending five-note scales*

Continue to as high, then as low, a note as comfortable; then repeat with other vowels.

Exercise 7.6 is designed to *improve your low range.* Remember to think of a heavier, yawnlike approach as you descend in pitch, but never force your voice.

Exercise 7.6   *Descending scale pattern*

Continue to as low a note as comfortable, then repeat with other vowels.

Exercise 7.7 is for *increasing your fortissimo ability.* As you strive for greater volume, remember to use the best possible *resonance*, not just breath power, to sing loudly. Work to achieve as much space and amplification as possible in your entire resonating system.

Exercise 7.7   *Ascending octave scale with crescendo*

Continue to as high a note as comfortable, then repeat with other vowels.

Increasing your pianissimo ability is the aim of Exercise 7.8, which is Exercise 7.7 with the dynamics reversed. It is one of the most effective devices for learning the control and coordination required for very soft singing. Take care not to sing this exercise higher than is comfortable for you.

Exercise 7.8   *Ascending octave scale with decrescendo*

Continue to as high a note as comfortable, then repeat with other vowels.

To develop your *vibrato*, first review the pulsation exercise in Chapter 2. Then, in Exercise 7.9, pulsate the three sets of four notes and let the natural vibrato take over on the long note. Try to pulsate as nearly as possible at the speed of a normal vibrato.

Exercise 7.9 *Single-tone pulsations with vibrato*

Continue ascending by half-steps, then repeat with other vowels.

Exercise 7.10 is practice in *legato* style. In spite of the intentionally awkward intervals in this exercise, make your moves from note to note smooth, graceful, and connected.

Exercise 7.10 *Legato leaps*

Repeat using other vowels.

Three exercises are given for *flexibility and agility*, vital parts of coordination building. They should all be sung slowly at first, building speed only as accuracy and precision can be maintained. In Exercise 7.11, keep each note very short, and use a light attack.

Exercise 7.11   *Staccato arpeggios*

Repeat using other vowels.

In Exercise 7.12 be sure you have enough "bounce" in each of the slurred notes to articulate each pitch clearly. Thinking of a very slight accent on each group of three will help.

Exercise 7.12   *Staccato-legato alternation*

Ascend entire sequence by half-steps. Repeat using other vowels.

Sing Exercise 7.13 first legato, then staccato. Use all vowels. Breathe only at the ends of phrases.

Exercise 7.13 *Sixteenth-note scale patterns*

Continue to as high a note as comfortable, then repeat with other vowels.

ASSIGNMENTS

Prepare your final song presentation (for performance following the next chapter). This should be a truly "finished product." Choose your piece carefully, making a selection that suits your voice and personality. Polish it as if you were to sing it in a formal recital. Make use of every element of knowledge and skill you have learned during the past weeks. Show the class and your instructor the progress you have made.

8

INTERPRETATION

EXPRESSIVE SINGING

Interpretation is an element of musical expression that all musicians share. It involves conveying the ideas of the composer to the audience in a personal, individual manner. All musical performances reflect the individuality of the performer, because expression of the music is ultimately that performer's *interpretation* of that music. Although the composer created the musical composition, it is the performer's concept of the composition that is delivered to the audience. For the singer, the interpretive assignment includes conveying the expressive ideas of not only the composer, but also a poet or an author.

Interpretation, like the more technical aspects of singing, requires skill. Interpretive skills, like technical skills, usually must be developed. In fact, they are developed in much the same way, through knowledge, understanding, guidance, and practice. The process of gaining knowledge and understanding began when you heard your first song; it continues with every new song and each performance you hear. Guidance is provided by your teacher, other singers, recordings, and even classmates. Practice is largely up to you.

It seems obvious that before you can interpret and convey to others the meaning of anything, you must understand it. Therefore it is only logical that you must thoroughly understand any song you sing, and you must have a definite concept of its meaning, musical as well as literal. You need to learn about the composer, the poet, the times in which they lived, and as much as possible about what they were trying to express. You should also know if there is a tradition about how the piece is usually sung, and, if so, why. You should look for predominant expressive elements—a prevailing mood or emotional attitude, for example. You should also observe any musical or technical difficulties that may affect your expressive potential. In short, to achieve an effective interpretation of a song, you need to explore every aspect of it in detail.

Once you have learned everything you can about a song, and have prepared it musically and vocally, it is yours to express to others. How is this done? How can you convey all the subtle, sometimes hidden meanings in the music and in the words to someone who doesn't already know what you know about the song? You do it with what are often called *expressive tools*. These are the musical and technical devices that enable singers to communicate effectively on a musical and emotional level. A few of these are: *dynamic contrast*, the ability to sing very softly or very loudly and to make these changes gradually or abruptly; *tone color*, the ability to sing with a bright timbre or a darker one to reflect different moods; *phrasing*, the choice of when to breathe for specific emphasis or to avoid a confusing rendering of the text; and *attack-release style*, the ability to sing in a detached, *staccato* manner of attacks and releases, or to connect words and pitches in a more sustained, *legato* manner. Virtually every vocal technique that has been covered in prior chapters, from breathing to articulation, is brought into play in achieving expressive singing. In addition there are important nonvocal elements, such as facial expressions and physical gestures.

As you work to develop your interpretive skills, seek the reactions of your teacher and your classmates about their effectiveness. Also carefully watch and listen to other singers, both live and on television and in films. Notice how they use their expressive tools. Don't attempt to copy or even imitate another interpretation of a song, however. Interpretations are unique. You are a unique person. Your interpretation will be successful only if it is uniquely yours. That of another singer is uniquely his or hers; it may or may not work well for that singer, but it almost certainly will not work as well for you as your own. Your interpretation will ring true and really communicate only if it reflects *your* personal feelings and emotions.

CONVEYING THE TEXT

Solo songs are among the most personal expressions in music literature. They are necessarily subjective, because the basis of their origin is a literary text. The text, in fact, is the most basic element of the composition and must be given first consideration when you are preparing to interpret the song. In the early stages of studying a song, you should consider the text carefully. Examine each thought and idea for inflection and inner meaning. As you explore the deepest dimensions of the text, you will apply certain connotations of your own that will ultimately shape your interpretation.

To communicate a song text effectively, you should express it in much the same way excellent actors deliver their lines. Obviously, articulation skills are essential. Even the most basic ideas of the text cannot be communicated if the words are not enunciated intelligibly. In addition, the text must be conveyed with expression. Stress must be placed upon key words. Phrases of special significance must be emphasized. If you do not do this, much of the potential meaning of the text is lost; certainly the emotion it can carry will be lost.

Read the following song text aloud, without reference to the music:

The Turtle Dove

Fare you well, my dear, I must be gone,
And leave you for awhile;
If I roam away I'll come back again,
Though I roam ten thousand miles, my dear,
Though I roam ten thousand miles.

So fair thou art my bonny lass,
So deep in love am I;
But I never will prove false to the bonny lass I love,
'Til the stars fall from the sky, my dear,
'Til the stars fall from the sky.

. . . .

O yonder doth sit that little turtle dove,
He doth sit on yonder high tree,
A-making a moan for the loss of his love,
As I will do for thee, my dear,
As I will do for thee.

Notice that, while it is a "period piece" from an earlier era, with language that may seem old fashioned, the feelings it expresses are as valid today as when they were written. Try to express these thoughts with sufficient feeling to convey the emotions the author felt. Make use of both a tape recorder and a mirror. Is your reading convincing? Are you conveying genuine feelings? Have you ever experienced a situation similar to the one the song relates? If not, can you imagine such a situation and sympathize with the participant's feelings? Until you can answer these questions affirmatively, continue to practice reading the text, before you even approach the music that goes with it.

When you feel that your text rendering is convincing, try it out on a small "audience"—a close friend or two, or perhaps another member of your voice class. Observe the listeners' reactions carefully. If you are successful, they will be moved. If they remain indifferent, you need to do more work.

Probably the most important point to remember in developing text expression skills is that you must be willing to *feel* as well as to convey emotion. If you are unable to relate to the emotions of the text, or if you are unwilling to express such feelings before an audience, your singing of emotional songs is not likely to be successful. If you find that personal inhibitions limit your text expression abilities, start with texts that are of a nonpersonal nature, and perfect a few of these. Then gradually try texts that are more and more emotional. If you are naturally inhibited, you may find this a very useful way to free yourself of many of your expressive inhibitions. In turn, the release of these inhibitions will enhance your development as an expressive singer.

MUSICAL STYLE

Expressing musical ideas accurately requires skills quite different from those needed for successfully conveying literary ideas. They are, nonetheless, expressive skills and are developed in much the same way, with knowledge, understanding, guidance, and practice. For many beginning singers, prior musical study may have been scant or even nonexistent. If this is true for you, and you are serious about training your voice, hasten to fill the void, for a well-developed singing voice is of little use if you do not understand music. A college music fundamentals class is a good place to begin this training, and private study of a musical instrument (perhaps piano) is an excellent way to continue. A music appreciation course will give you a general overview of the history of music and some concepts of musical style.

Musical style is a matter of considerable importance in successful interpretation of songs. If you are particularly interested in country and western music you do not want to hear it sung in operatic style. The result would be atrocious (as would the reverse). A blues singer has a very different style from a rock singer. A singer of art songs does not even sing the music of Mozart the same way he sings the music of Brahms. Obviously, to interpret any style of music, the performer must first understand that style. This necessitates thorough exploration of the music you sing. You need to experience performances of similar material by established artists and to study your particular songs very carefully.

Some interpretive directions are usually given in the music by the composer: *tempo*, the speed of the basic pulse; *dynamics*, the levels of loudness; *style of attack and release*, the detached or connected flow of notes; and sometimes *phrasing indications*, when to breathe. Frequently all these directions are given in Italian. If not, they will probably be given in the composer's native language. Therefore you should purchase a small pocket dictionary of musical terms. It will prove useful again and again in your quest to become an expressive singer.

Many facets of musical style cannot be successfully communicated on the printed musical score. Instead they become stylistic traditions that are carried on by the performers themselves. Novices learn them either by explicit teaching or simply from hearing performances. One of these concepts is the horizontal contour a musical phrase must have—its sense of "going somewhere." This concept cannot be successfully conveyed on the printed page; it must be learned by experience. Similarly, many subtle musical nuances cannot be adequately verbalized, yet they are important expressive devices and contribute greatly to the interpretation of a song. At these sophisticated levels of musical expression, you will achieve skills only after considerable exposure to a wide range of music.

Keep in mind that, if your intellectual and emotional understanding of a song is clear, you can convey the intent of the composer effectively. If your interpretation stems from a distinct inner conception of the music, it will very likely be a sincere one and will arouse the emotions of your audience.

even more interested in singing now than when you began and more enthusiastic about continuing to use and develop your singing voice.

This course has been little more than a starting point, a foundation, designed to acquaint you with the basic elements of voice training. Your instructor and this text have tried to describe and illustrate for you the basic anatomy of the singing instrument and to explain its physiology. We have tried to help you establish healthy, constructive physical habits for singing and eradicate any destructive ones you had already established. We have provided productive vocalises and exercises to help you build your voice, begin to gain mastery of it, and maintain it. We have tried to impart a body of knowledge about how to perform successfully, whatever your choice of musical material. We have sought to teach you the essentials required of a singer. As a result, we hope (and expect) that you have made some exciting new discoveries. Friends and acquaintances who hear you sing have probably already noticed a significant improvement in your vocal quality and performance skills. We expect that you will want to continue to train your voice after you finish this course.

If these last statements are true for you (and we anticipate that they will be) you have undoubtedly already realized that training the voice, like developing most physical arts, is not an overnight process. Indeed, for the average person it takes many years of study to acquire the vocal and musical skills to become a successful singer. Also, depending on your present age, the chances are that your vocal instument is not even physically mature yet. Voices, on the average, continue to undergo natural physical changes and growth until about the middle twenties—often even later, especially among males. It is frequently said that singers are the only musicians who must continue to *construct* their instrument as they learn to play it. All of these circumstances indicate the necessity for further study, if you seek full development of your voice.

If this course has helped you realize some of your vocal potential and you are encouraged by its possibilities, you have probably already considered further training of some kind. There are two logical alternatives: continued group study in an advanced voice class, and private instruction. Each has certain advantages.

An advanced voice class will continue, more or less, where this one concluded. It will probably be smaller, allowing more individual attention from the instructor, and it will retain most of the initial advantages of group study: learning with (and from) others and having their support and encouragement; being able to receive frequent critical review; and having the inspiration and incentive offered by classmates' vocal progress. It will undoubtedly delve deeper into each of the areas introduced in this course, from breathing to interpretation. Probably a great deal of emphasis will be placed on performance. Your chances to perform will probably be more frequent than during the present course, and the instructor will expect more vocal, musical, and interpretive skill from you. Finally—a very practical consideration—the advanced class is likely to be far less expensive than private lessons. In short, the advanced voice class is an excellent way to continue what you began in this course. If you found the attributes of group study to your liking, you will probably derive a great deal from the same approach on an advanced level.

On the other hand, if you have felt during this course that the class approach limits the speed of your progress, or in any other way confines you, you may wish to explore private instruction. Working one-to-one with a private teacher is quite a different experience from participating in class study. Since you have the teacher's undivided attention, it is somewhat more intense—you are "in the spotlight" throughout each session. Since private sessions are usually shorter than class sessions (generally thirty minutes for beginning students) and meet less frequently (usually only once per week), you must accomplish much more on your own. For these reasons you must be capable of self-discipline or you will not make satisfactory progress. The most crucial aspect of studying privately is finding a good teacher. Voice teachers, unfortunately, are not required to be licensed, certified, or officially approved in any other way in order to pursue their profession, and there is a disturbing number of unqualified ones "teaching." There are also many skilled, dedicated, and highly qualified professionals. Your voice is precious; it is the only one you will ever have. You should select your voice teacher with the same care as you would your doctor or dentist. How do you go about making such a choice? How can an inexperienced student determine if a voice teacher is a *good* one?

CHOOSING A TEACHER OR COACH

First it is important to understand the distinction between a voice *teacher* and a voice *coach.* Although the two terms are sometimes used interchangeably, they really describe two different kinds of teaching activity. Voice teachers are concerned primarily with developing the singer's instrument, that is, the voice itself. Teachers are responsible for teaching the singer the technical skills necessary to produce a beautiful, healthy tone; to sing on pitch, with a wide range of dynamic and other expressive qualities; and to establish good habits for continued growth and maintenance of the voice. In addition, good and thorough voice teachers often assume some of the duties of voice coaches.

Voice coaches are more concerned with proper execution of vocal *music* than with the technical aspects of tone production. They must have a thorough understanding of correct vocal technique, although they need not be singers personally. (Most vocal coaches, in fact, begin their training as accompanists.) But their special skills are with diction (they should be experts on the correct lyric diction for English, Italian, German, French, and possibly Spanish), musical style of all musical periods (they should have a sound historical knowledge of musical styles, both vocal and instrumental); and repertoire selection (they must have a vast knowledge of the vocal repertoire for the genre they coach, whether opera, art songs, popular music, or musical comedy).

In short, voice teachers, first and foremost, train the *voice;* they teach the student a singing *technique.* Voice coaches, first and foremost, train the *singer;* they endeavor to turn correct vocal technique into artistic *singing.* They help the singer to sing expressively, musically, and in a stylistically correct manner. Vocal coaches are usually sought by more advanced singers who have already established a good singing technique. Once the student is singing consistently well and is ready for public performance, a vocal coach can be of invaluable assistance in achieving truly artistic singing. For the beginning singer (or one who has just finished a beginning voice class such as this one), the voice *teacher* is the logical choice.

How can you be sure the teacher you select will guide your vocal development properly? After all, it is *your* voice (and your money!); the teacher who trains it must be not only competent but also the right teacher for *you*.

One criterion commonly used for assessing a teacher's competence is his or her reputation as a *singer*. It seems to be widely believed that a fine performer will quite naturally also be a fine teacher. Unfortunately, this is often not the case. Most successful professional singers have neither the time nor the inclination to make the commitment to teaching required of a truly dedicated teacher. Performers are performers because performing is their first love (just as the first love of most excellent teachers is teaching rather than performing). Also, if performers had a natural talent, so that much of their singing skill came very easily, they probably did not have to deal with many of the usual problems of the average voice, and they lack firsthand understanding of such problems. It is, however, important that a teacher be a *competent* singer; accurate demonstration of production techniques is an essential teaching tool. But having a successful singing career has little to do with ability to teach fundamental singing techniques effectively. Probably the worst candidates for teachers are singers whose careers (and/or voices) failed, or those who aspired to a singing career but never "made it." Both categories of singers choose teaching as a last resort, a source of livelihood to "fall back on," not a first choice made for a love of teaching, or an inborn desire to share knowledge. This is not to say that such individuals cannot become good teachers, just that it is less likely that they will be as successful as individuals who choose teaching in the first place, due to an innate desire and need to do so.

Perhaps an even more common basis for choosing a voice teacher is the performing skills and reputations of some of his or her outstanding students. At first this seems a valid method. After all, if a given teacher has not one or two but several highly successful students, doesn't it stand to reason that his or her teaching methods are superior? Not necessarily. It probably means that the teaching methods are not harmful, but it still does not mean this is the best teacher for a beginner or near-beginner. Studio teachers working in a college, university, or conservatory setting normally enjoy a clientele of students with better-than-average vocal talent (that is, musical background, singing experience, and natural coordination). Some of these voices are so strong, healthy, and secure that they would survive even poor teaching techniques (although in most colleges, universities, and conservatories, poor teaching is unlikely). Indeed, many highly successful professional singers have escaped relatively unscathed from some pretty questionable teaching methods. So, even finding that a number of outstanding singers come from a given studio is not the best criterion for selecting that teacher.

The best method is a sure one, but certainly not the easiest to apply. It is to seek a teacher who has proved successful time and again in developing good singers from average or below-average vocal potential. Such a teacher is most likely to succeed with anyone, including you—whatever your present attributes. Finding such a teacher will more than likely require some serious investigation—particularly if he or she doesn't have a flock of famous students. You will need to ask in your local community all those who have knowledge of voice teachers and voice students: singers, both professional and amateur, choral directors, high school and college music departments, and so forth. Van A. Christy has suggested seven "Indications of Good Teaching" that you should keep in mind during your quest. The voice teacher you seek should:

Most ga
contain
flammat
alcohol)

Exc
speaking
the high
speakers
effort to
treatme
in song.
is to rea
are pote
long per
If you w
excessiv

Sin
weather
maining
colds to
have a
making
at wors
isolated
vocal st

The
show m
singer's
utterly
Muscul
so forth
artistic
tern of
a perfo
relaxat
crucial
you for
mainte

Yo
staying
good vo
you ma
to con
further
the ski
vocal
expect

1. Have extensive experience with beginning students.

2. Have demonstrated consistently successful results with all types of students, particularly those in the beginning level.

3. Have particular success in training students who are recognized as having had poor voices. (This is a high test of teaching ability.)

4. Having personally overcome many technical and, perhaps, physical difficulties, learning to sing the hard way. (NOTE: Not an absolute requirement but a situation favorable to understanding a wide variety of vocal problems.)

5. Have the habit of emphasizing ease and quality, not quantity of voice. To judge the worth of any particular method or idea expounded by a teacher, apply the test of ease. If production appears to sound and feel more strained, it is wrong; if easier, you are likely to be on the right track.

6. Have the habit of emphasizing expression first and technique second.

7. Have the educational philosophy of guiding and challenging students to think for themselves, to use their intelligence and emotions in evolving interpretations; is not autocratic in insisting that there is only one way to interpret a song—the teacher's way.[1]

Dr. Christy also gives excellent advice on the kinds of teachers to avoid:

1. AVOID the teacher who insists continually on *fortissimo* singing.

2. AVOID study with an opera or professional singer whose voice lasted only a short time, forcing them to teach for a livelihood. They will most likely transmit the very faults which shortened their careers, since that is all they know. (On the other hand, after the voice is safely matured, a person with this background may make an excellent coach in the repertoire of their experience.)

3. AVOID the teacher who assigns demanding operatic arias of *fortissimo* dramatic songs with wide range in the first year of study, or at any time before the voice is free and even over an adequate range.

4. AVOID teachers whose students all sound alike—they are slavishly imitating their teacher, an unwise and dangerous procedure.

5. AVOID teachers whose students, although still in their teens or early twenties, sound as mature and powerful as voices in their forties. *A young voice should sound young*, maturity should be gradual and natural, not forced.[2]

Above all, don't choose your voice teacher hastily, without careful and deliberate consideration. Your singing future can be ruined by a poor or unqualified teacher. You have every right to be very selective.

MAINTAINING YOUR VOICE

Whether you continue study with a private teacher, choose an advanced voice class, or don't continue formal training at all, you will certainly want to maintain all the

---

1. Van A. Christy, *Expressive Singing*, 3d ed., 2 vols. (Dubuque, Iowa: Wm. C. Brown, 1967), 1:17. Used by permission.
2. Ibid. Used by permission.

YOUR VOCAL FUTURE

What do you want to do with your voice now? Have your singing aspirations changed since you began this course? Perhaps you have discovered that you have more vocal talent than you suspected. Or you may have realized that singing well requires more time, practice, patience, discipline, and so forth than you are able to devote to it. In any case, you have undoubtedly noticed that singing can offer some satisfaction to almost everyone, whether it is pursued purely for personal pleasure or chosen as a professional career. Obviously the career singer will have to devote a vastly greater amount of time, energy, discipline, money, and the like to voice study than the singer who develops his or her voice primarily for recreation. This does not mean that the pleasure to be derived from singing is necessarily greater for one than for the other, or for those at the many other levels between these two extremes of vocal ambition. Perhaps you enjoy choral singing and would find satisfaction and pleasure singing in a fine church choir, community chorus, or college or university choral ensemble while you are in school. If theater interests you, musical comedy opportunities abound in most communities for those with voice training. You may wish to pursue folk-singing, or country and western music. You might choose to join a rock or pop band or to involve yourself in some other kind of musical entertainment. The possibilities for making pleasurable and satisfying use of your singing skills are virtually endless if you have sufficient desire to do so.

The degree to which you engage in singing activities in the future is directly related to this desire. Career singers must *need* to sing so intensely that they are willing to work very hard and sacrifice many other things in life to achieve success as performers. They must accept the fact that competition is very keen in nearly all fields of professional singing—so keen, in fact, that only a small percentage of those who train for such careers are able to earn a good living from them. They must be willing, even eager, to compete. They must be able to deal with rejection, even failure, without giving up. In short, their desire to sing must be great enough to make them strong, competitive, and resilient. Successful career singers nearly always have these qualities. Individuals who sing primarily for personal pleasure—perhaps for the entertainment of close friends, or an occasional performance before a large audience—obviously have fewer demands to satisfy than career singers. They enjoy the activity and derive pleasure from it, but their *need* to sing for the public is less urgent. They are probably less willing to make substantial sacrifices for the art, because other pursuits in their lives have equal or greater importance.

The intensity of your desire to sing will dictate the level of involvement that is right for you. If you have discovered that you *must* be a singer and your vocal potential justifies considering a singing career, you may wish to know more about what is involved in different singing fields. Opera singers, for example, are considered by many people to have the most highly developed voices. This is because opera requires extraordinary vocal resources for a single, unamplified voice to project above some-times gigantic orchestral and choral forces. The voice must be not only powerful but also beautiful. Achieving such vocal development takes many years of tireless exercise and study, relentless dedication, and a great deal of patience. Even then, only a small number of "stars" earn a large, steady income in this field. Most opera singers must supplement their incomes with nonoperatic engagements—appearances as soloists with orchestras and choruses, recitals, and the like. Yet the rewards for the few who are highly successful are abundant—there are probably no fans more devoted and demonstrative than opera fans! You should not even consider a career as an opera singer, however, unless your vocal gifts are formidable. For each singer who succeeds in this field, hundreds fail.

A full-time career as a concert singer or recitalist in this country is virtually impossible at present, because the population that is musically sophisticated enough to support such events is too small. Most recitalists are also opera singers or soloists who perform frequently with orchestras and choruses. Only a singer already successful enough to have a "name" is likely to attract a significant audience for a solo recital in this country. This unfortunate phenomenon accounts for the diminishing interest in art songs and other solo recital literature among the general population. However, the solo recital is an important means for successful career singers to supplement their income, and this keeps alive the literature in the genre.

The musical theater has attracted an abundance of fine voices in recent years. Vocal demands are not as great as those for operatic singing, but great emphasis is placed on dramatic skills. The performer's voice must be capable of going from song to speech without abrupt changes in placement or quality. In opera the leading characters often have the highest voices; in musical theater the leads usually have middle-range voices, while character parts are usually given to singers with the highest and lowest voices. Since musical theater productions are usually amplified to some degree, singers are not required to develop the volume and projecting power needed by opera singers. Consequently, musical theater singers sound more "natural" to many people, and the general public has (at least at present) a greater appreciation for musicals than for opera. Because of the enormous popularity of musical comedy in this country, and the resultant abundance of opportunities for singing actors, this field is a very important one for those considering a singing career.

There are certainly many other performance opportunities for trained voices: church choir soloist positions, professional choruses (such as those that perform with major symphony orchestras), opera choruses, musical theater choruses, and so forth. While these engagements do not usually provide an adequate total income, they are highly desirable for those who have other sources of income, but still want some kind of singing career.

Popular forms of vocal music, particularly pop, rock, and country, have created a relatively new kind of singing "star"—the recording artist. However, since "style" and the musical arrangement nearly always take precedence over vocal quality in these forms, serious vocal training seldom pertains to a singer's chance for success. Probably of much greater importance are skill as an entertainer, successful organization and management of the backup musicians, promotion, "connections" within the music business, the current whim of the public, and luck. That is not to say that vocal training is of no use to recording artists. Probably its greatest value is to teach them to *protect* their most valuable commodity. In fact, if more popular singers studied voice, the quality of pop, rock, country, and other singing would undoubtedly improve, and fewer such singers would end their careers while still in their youth.

CONCLUSION

At the outset of this text we suggested that an excellent way to stimulate your self-motivation for consistent vocal development was to explore *all kinds of singing*. If you have done that throughout this course, you have probably contemplated some new avenues of singing possibilities. You may have even come to appreciate certain kinds of singing you didn't care for previously. Certainly you have learned some things about *all* kinds of singing that were unfamiliar before. From these experiences, the experiences you had before coming into this course, and the experiences of the course itself, you now have a clearer concept of your own vocal abilities and perhaps of your singing ambitions. Only you can determine how to use your singing voice in the future. It may become an integral part of your daily existence or only a recreational outlet. You alone will decide how and to what extent you make use of it. However you choose to use it, take great pride in your ownership of it and the skills you now possess, marvel at its possibilities, cherish its beauty, protect it from harm, and, above all, *enjoy* it.

SONG
ANTHOLOGY

INTRODUCTION
TO THE SONGS

The songs in this anthology have
been selected to serve a variety of
needs, because students in voice
classes have diverse musical back-
grounds, interests, and goals. You
may wish to improve your voice, but
not necessarily for the purpose of
singing art songs. Therefore, re-
hearsing and preparing art songs
may not help you reach your artistic
goal. Yet many art songs are very effective vehicles for vocal development. Preparing a few may not only
assist you in developing a sound
vocal technique but also expand
your musical horizons. You may discover a body of satisfying musical
literature that you never knew ex-
isted before. It is simply not true
that vocal improvement can take
place *only* with a steady diet of
"classical" songs, however. Many
fine voices have been developed with
virtually none. This song collection
is presented with the attitude that

teaching materials in a *variety* of musical styles will meet a wide range of individual needs and tastes, and each individual's singing experience will be enhanced by learning a variety of song genres.

Not all of the songs presented here are intended for beginners. Certain of the art songs, operatic arias, and duets in particular require some training and facility. While no composition in this anthology is exceedingly difficult, some demand skills greater than those usually acquired in a beginning voice course. Such songs have been included for students who have already had some prior study and students using this textbook in second- or third-level voice classes. These songs offer material for future study by beginning students as well.

Your instructor is your best guide about which songs are most appropriate for your level of development. Be sure to check with him or her before you begin preparing any song. Where a song is presented in more than one key, again consult your teacher about which is best for you. (You may be straining on pitches too high or two low for you and not even realize it, if you are caught up in the beauty of a melody or a profound expressive idea.)

Finally, the songs have been chosen for their considerable aesthetic qualities and broad appeal. While you will be able to prepare only a few during this class, we hope that many more will appeal to you and that you will pursue some of them after the course is over. Thoroughly enjoy the music, and take advantage of every opportunity these songs offer you to improve your vocal skills.

AMARILLI, MIA BELLA

Amarilli, My Fair One

LOW VOICE

English by
Dr. Theodore Baker

Giulio Caccini
(1546–1618)

AMARILLI, MIA BELLA

Amarilli, My Fair One

HIGH VOICE

English by
Dr. Theodore Baker

Giulio Caccini
(1546–1618)

mor t'as - sa - le,   du - bi-tar non ti va - le.
fear as - sail   thee,   It can nev - er a - vail thee.

dolce
p

f   *p*

A -   pri-mi il pet - to e ve-drai scrit-to in co - re: A - ma-
Ope   thou my bo - som, and see thy fears re-prov - ed;   On my

f   *p*   *smorz.*   *dolce*

cresc.   *più cresc.*

ril - li,   A - ma - ril - li,   A - ma-
heart 'tis_ writ,   On my heart 'tis_ writ: "A - ma-

pp   *cresc.*   *più cresc.*

f   *poco rit.*   *a tempo*   *mf*

ril - li è il mio a - mo - re.   Cre - di-lo pur: e se ti-
ril - li, my be - lov - ed!"   Do but be-lieve,   for should e'er

a tempo
f   *poco rit.*   *p dolce*

mor t'as-sa - le,   du - bi-tar non ti va - le.   A - pri-mi il
fear as-sail thee,   It can nev-er a - vail thee.   Ope thou my

pet - to e ve-drai scrit-to in co - re: A-ma-ril - li,   A-ma-
bo - som, and see thy fears re-prov - ed;   On my heart 'tis_ writ,   On my

ril - li,   A-ma-ril - li è il mio a-mo - re;   A-ma-
heart 'tis_ writ: "A-ma-ril - li, my be-lov - ed;   A-ma-

ril - li_____ è il mio a-mo - re.
ril - li,_____ my be-lov - ed!"

AND WOULD YOU SEE MY MISTRESS' FACE

LOW VOICE

Philip Rosseter
(c. 1575–1623)

It is a sweet delicious morn
Where day is breeding, never born.
It is a meadow yet unshorn
Whom thousand flowers do adorn.

It is the heavens' bright reflex,
Weak eyes to dazzle and to vex;
It is the Idaea of her sex,
Envy of whom doth world perplex.

It is a face of death that smiles,
Pleasing, though it kills the whiles,
Where death and love in pretty wiles
Each other naturally beguiles.

It is fair beauty's freshest youth,
It is the feigned Elysium's truth,
The Spring that wintered hearts reneweth;
And this is that my soul pursueth.

AND WOULD YOU SEE MY MISTRESS' FACE

HIGH VOICE

Philip Rosseter
(c. 1575–1623)

It is a sweet delicious morn
Where day is breeding, never born.
It is a meadow yet unshorn
Whom thousand flowers do adorn.

It is the heavens' bright reflex,
Weak eyes to dazzle and to vex;
It is the Idaea of her sex,
Envy of whom doth world perplex.

It is a face of death that smiles,
Pleasing, though it kills the whiles,
Where death and love in pretty wiles
Each other naturally beguiles.

It is fair beauty's freshest youth,
It is the feigned Elysium's truth,
The Spring that wintered hearts reneweth;
And this is that my soul pursueth.

BREAKE NOW MY HEART AND DYE

Thomas Campian
(1567–1620)

Breake now my heart and dye, Oh no, oh no, she may re - lent.
Let my de-spaire pre - vayle, oh stay, oh stay, hope is not spent.

Should she now fixe____ one smile on thee, where were de-spaire?

The losse is but eas - ie which smiles can re - payre.
A stran - ger would please thee, if she were as fayre.

Her must I love or none, so sweet none breathes as shee,
The more is my despayre, alas she loves not me:
But cannot time make way for love through ribs of steele?
  The Grecian inchanted all parts but the heele,
  At last a shafte daunted which his hart did feele.

DA UNTEN IM TALE

The Stream in the Valley

LOW VOICE

English by Charles Edward Lindsley

Johannes Brahms (1833–1897)
Edited by Charles Edward Lindsley

3. Und wenn i dirs zehn - mal sag, dass ich dich
3. If I say ten times o - ver I love you, I

4. Für die Zeit, wo du g'liebt mi hast, dank i dir
4. For the time that you loved me I gave you my

lieb,____ und du willst nit ver - ste - hen, muss
know,____ will you say that you love me? If

schön,____ und i wünsch, dass dirs an-ders-wo
heart,____ But I know that it's o - ver and

i haltweiter gehn.
not, I will go.

bes - ser mag gehn.
now we must part.

DA UNTEN IM TALE

The Stream in the Valley

HIGH VOICE

English by Charles Edward Lindsley

Johannes Brahms (1833–1897)
Edited by Charles Edward Lindsley

3. Und wenn i dirs zehn - mal sag, dass i di lieb, und du
3. *If I say ten times o - ver I love you, I know will you*

4. Für die Zeit, wo du g'liebt mi hast, dank i dir schön, und i
4. *For the time that you loved me I gave you my heart, But I*

dim.

willst nit ver - ste - hen muss i halt weiter - gehn.
say that you love me? If not, I will go.

wünsch, dass dirs an - ders - wo bes - ser mag gehn.
know that it's o - ver and now we must part.

FROM FAR, FROM EVE AND MORNING

A. E. Housman

Ralph Vaughan Williams (1872–1958)

Paul Bourget
Translated by Isa...

Copyright 1937 by
permission of the...

MADRIGAL

Dans le Style Ancien
(Madrigal in the Old Style)

Robert De Bonnières
English by Charles Edward Lindsley

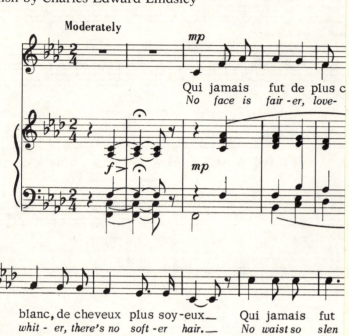

Qui jamais fut de plus c
No face is fair-er, love-

blanc, de cheveux plus soy-eux___ Qui jamais fut
whit-er, there's no soft-er hair.___ No waist so slen

Qui jamais fut que ma Dame aux doux yeux!
No-one has eyes like my love-gen-tle, fair!

ten -
tranc -

Qui j
No

fut
la -

ROMANCE

HIGH VOICE

Paul Bourget
Translated by Isabella G. Parker

Claude Achille Debussy
(1862–1918)

L'âme é-va-po-rée et souf-fran - te. L'â-me
Soul of light-est breath, soft-ly sail - ing, Soul so

dou-ce, l'â-me o-do-ran-te Des lis di-vins___ que j'ai cueillis Dans le jar-din de ta pen-
gen-tle, per-fume ex-hal-ing Of lil-y fair,___ the pre-cious dower Of thy dear thought, a gar-den

sée, Ou donc les vents l'ontils chassée, Cette âme a-do-ra-ble des
gay, Ah, whith-er is it borne a-way, This soul so di-vine of a

TU LO SAI
Ask Thy Heart

LOW VOICE

English by
Everett Helm

Giuseppe Torelli
(1650–1703)

Tu lo___ sai Quan-to t'a-mai,___ Tu lo___ sai, lo sai cru-del!___ Io non bra-mo al-tra mer-cè Ma ri-cor-da-ti di me,

Ask thy___ heart How I a-dore thee, Ask thy___ heart, O cru-el and fair!___ Oth-er plea-sure I do not crave Than thou think-est___ once on me,

*The following introduction may be used if desired:

TU LO SAI

Ask Thy Heart

HIGH VOICE

English by
Everett Helm

Giuseppe Torelli
(1650–1703)

*The following introduction may be used if desired:

VOLKSLIEDCHEN
Little Folk Song

LOW VOICE

F. Rückert
English by Charles Edward Lindsley

Robert Schumann (1810–1856)
Edited by Charles Edward Lindsley

Wenn ich früh in den Gar-ten geh' in mei-nem grü-nen Hut, ist mein
Morn - ing comes and I'm in the gar-den wear-ing my hat of green, And the

er - ster Ge - dan - ke, was nun mein Lieb-ster tut, ist mein
first thought I have is: How much to me you mean, And the

er - ster Ge - dan - ke, was nun mein Lieb - ster tut?
first thought I have is: How much to me you mean!

VOLKSLIEDCHEN
Little Folk Song

HIGH VOICE

F. Rückert
English by Charles Edward Lindsley

Robert Schumann (1810–1856)
Edited by Charles Edward Lindsley

Moderately fast

Wenn ich früh in den Gar-ten geh' in mei-nem grü-nen Hut, ist mein
Morn - ing comes and I'm in the gar - den, wear-ing my hat of green, And the

er-ster Ge -dan-ke, was nun mein Lieb-ster tut?
first thought I have is: How much to me you mean!

Am Him-mel steht kein Stern, den ich dem Freund nicht gönn - te. Mein
All hea-ven's stars you'd have, if they were mine to give you. My

Herz gäb' ich ihm gern, wenn ich's her - aus - tun könn - te.
heart I'd give you too if yours to me you'll give, too.

Wenn ich früh in den Gar-ten geh' in mei-nem grü-nen Hut, ist mein
Morn- ing comes and I 'm in the gar- den wear-ing my hat of green, And the

er - ster Ge- dan -ke, was nun mein Lieb- ster tut, ist mein
first thought I have is: How much to me you mean, And the

er - ster Ge- dan -ke, was nun mein Lieb - ster tut?
first thought I have is How much to me you mean !

WIE UNGLÜCKLICH BIN ICH NIT

How Sad Is My Lonely Heart

LOW VOICE

Anonymous
English by Charles Edward Lindsley

Wolfgang Amadeus Mozart (1756–1791)
Edited by Charles Edward Lindsley

Wie un-glück-lich bin ich nit, wie schmach-tend sind mei-ne Tritt, wenn ich mich nach dir
How sad is my lonely heart. Oh why did we have to part, when all life's joys seemed

len - ke.   Nur die Seuf-zer trö-sten mich, al - le Schmer-zen häu -fen sich, wenn
sure and true?   Now I'm left to grieve and mourn; all my hap-pi-ness is gone. I

ich auf dich ge-den-ke,   wenn ich auf dich ge-den - ke.
nev-er shall for-get you, I nev - er shall-for-get you.

WIE UNGLÜCKLICH BIN ICH NIT

How Sad Is My Lonely Heart

HIGH VOICE

Anonymous
English by Charles Edward Lindsley

Wolfgang Amadeus Mozart (1756–1791)
Edited by Charles Edward Lindsley

Adagio

Wie un - glück - lich bin ich nit, wie schmach - tend sind mei - ne Tritt; wenn ich mich nach dir
How sad is my lone - ly heart. Oh why did we have to part, when all life's joys seemed

len - ke. Nur die Seuf - zer trö - sten mich, al - le Schmer - zen häu - fen sich, wenn
sure and true? Now I'm left to grieve and mourn; all my hap - pi ness is gone. I

ich auf dich ge - den - ke, wenn ich auf dich ge - den - ke.
nev - er shall for - get you, I nev er shall for - get you.

WILLOW SONG

LOW VOICE

Anonymous (Seventeenth Century)
Edited by Charles Edward Lindsley

1. The poor soul sat sigh-ing   by a syc - a - more
2. He sighed in his sing-ing   and made a great

tree;   Sing wil - low, wil- low, wil-low,   With his hand on his
moan   Sing wil - low, wil- low, wil-low,   I am dead to all

bo - som and his head up- on his knee. O wil - low, wil-low, wil-low wil-low, O
plea-sure, my true love she is__ gone. O wil - low, wil-low, wil-low wil-low, O

1.2. wil-low, wil - low, wil-low, wil-low shall be my gar - land. Sing all a green

wil - low, wil - low, wil -low, wil - low. Ah

me, sing green wil - low must be my gar - land.

WILLOW SONG

HIGH VOICE

Anonymous (Seventeenth Century)
Edited by Charles Edward Lindsley

1. The poor soul sat sigh-ing by a syc - a-more
2. He sighed in his sing-ing and made a great

tree;   Sing wil - low, wil- low, wil - low,   With his
moan;   Sing wil - low, wil-llow, wil - low,   I am

hand on his bo - som and his head up-on his knee. O wil-low, wil-low, wil-low,
dead to all pleas-ure, my true love she is __ gone. O wil-low, wil-low, wil-low,

BLACK IS THE COLOR
OF MY TRUE LOVE'S HAIR

LOW VOICE

Collected and arranged by
John Jacob Niles

love___ the grass where - on she stands.

mf

I___ love my_ love and_ well she knows, I

love___ the grass where - on she goes; If___ she on___ earth no___

* Troublesome Creek, which empties into the Kentucky River.

Black, black, black is the col-or of my true love's hair, Her lips _____ are some-thing ro-sy fair, The _____ pert-est_ face and the dain-ti-est_ hands— I love_____ the grass where-on she stands.

BLACK IS THE COLOR
OF MY TRUE LOVE'S HAIR

HIGH VOICE

Collected and arranged by
John Jacob Niles

love___ the grass where - on she stands.

I ___ love my___ love and well she knows, I

love_____ the grass where - on she goes; If___ she on___ earth no___

more__ I__ see, My life____ will quick-ly leave me.

I__ go to_Troub-le-some* to mourn, to weep, But

sat - is-fied I ne'er can sleep; I'll__ write her a note in__

a few lit - tle lines, I'll suf - fer death ten thou-sand times.

*Troublesome Creek, which empties into the Kentucky River.

Black, black, black is the col-or of my true love's hair, Her lips_____ are some-thing ro-sy fair, The__ pert-est_ face and the dain-ti-est_ hands— I love____ the grass where-on she stands.

DANNY BOY
(Eily Dear)
LOW VOICE

Fred. E. Weatherly

Adapted from an
Old Irish Air
by Fred. E. Weatherly

Oh, Dan-ny Boy, } the pipes, the pipes are call - ing.......... From glen to
Oh, Ei - ly dear, }

glen,   and down the moun - tain   side,................. The sum - mer's

hear, though soft you tread a - bove..... me,................ And all my

grave will warm - er, sweet - er be,....................... For you will

sempre pp f

poco rit.

bend and tell me that you love..... me,................ And I shall

sempre pp

poco cresc e rit.

a little slower

più lento.

rall.

sleep in peace un - til you come to me!...

più lento.

rall.

ppp

DANNY BOY

HIGH VOICE

Fred. E. Weatherly

Adapted from an
Old Irish Air
by Fred. E. Weatherly

Oh, Dan-ny Boy, the pipes, the pipes are call - ing — From glen to glen, and down the moun-tain side, — The sum-mer's

gone, and all the ro-ses fall-ing,— It's you, it's you must go, and I must

bide.— But come ye back when sum-mer's in the mea-dow,— Or when the

val-ley's hushed and white with snow,— It's I'll be here in sun-shine or in

sha-dow,— Oh, Dan-ny Boy, oh, Dan-ny Boy, I love you so!—

hear, though soft you tread a - bove me, ___ And all my

grave will warm - er, sweet - er be, ___ For you will

bend and tell me that you love ___ me, ___ And I shall

sleep in peace un - til you come to me! ___

DRINK TO ME ONLY WITH THINE EYES

LOW VOICE

Ben Jonson   Old English Song

Drink to me on-ly with-thine eyes, And I-will pledge with mine;—

Or leave a kiss with-in——the cup——and I'll—not ask for wine.—— The

thirst—that from the soul—doth rise doth ask a drink di-vine——

But might I of Jove's nec-tar sup,—I would not change for thine.——

DRINK TO ME ONLY WITH THINE EYES

HIGH VOICE

Ben Jonson   Old English Song

Drink to me on - ly with thine eyes, and I__ will pledge with mine;__

Or leave a kiss with - in__ the cup__ and I'll__ not ask for wine._____ The

thirst__ that from the soul__ doth rise doth ask a drink__ di - vine;

But might I of Jove's nec - tar sup,__ I would__ not change for thine.____

I sent thee late a ro - sy wreath, Not so_ much hon - 'ring thee_

As giv - ing it a hope_that there_ it could_ not with - er'd be.___ But

thou_ there - on didst on - ly breathe, And send'st it back_ to me,___

Since when it grows, and smells,_ I swear,_ Not of_ it - self, but thee!_

HE'S THE LILY OF THE VALLEY

HIGH VOICE

Traditional Black Spiritual
Arranged by Charles Edward Lindsley

Oh, my Lord, (1) With six white hor-ses side by side, Oh, my
(2) To glo-ry there for all to see,

Lord. He's the Li-ly of the Val-ley,— Oh, my Lord. He's the

Li-ly of the Val-ley,— Oh, my Lord.

MY LADY GREENSLEEVES

John Irvine

Old English Melody
arranged by
Roger Quilter (1877–1953)

NOBODY KNOWS THE TROUBLE I SEE

LOW VOICE

American Negro Melody
Arranged by J. Rosamond Johnson

*) In the original Folksong this line reads "Nobody knows but Jesus," which may be used when suitable.

trou_ble I see, No_bod_y knows my sor_row,— No_bod_y knows the trou_ble I see,

f *mf mournfully*

Glo _ ry Hal_le _ lu _ jah! Oh, Lord, the trou_ble I see, No_bod_y knows my

Little by little slower & lower faster

poco a poco rall. e cresc. ff allargando

sor _ row,— No_bod_y knows the trou_ble I see, Glo _ ry Hal _ le _

poco a poco rall. cresc. allargando ff

* *pp* *slowly and very softly* *pp*

_ lu _ jah! Oh, no_bod_y knows the trou_ble I see, No_bod_y knows my sor _ row.

pp pp ppp

* Singers who prefer to do so may end here, with a pause on the final note and chord.

NOBODY KNOWS THE TROUBLE I SEE

HIGH VOICE

American Negro Melody
Arranged by J. Rosamond Johnson

★ Singers who prefer to do so may end here, with a pause on the final note and chord.

O WALY, WALY

Cecil Sharp   Benjamin Britten (1913–1976)

From *Folk Song Arrangements, Vol. 3* © Copyright 1947
by Boosey & Co., Ltd.; renewed 1975. Reprinted by
permission of Boosey & Hawkes, Inc.

flowers both red and blue, I lit-tle thought what love can do.
deep as the love I'm in: I know not if I sink or swim.

O, love is hand- -some and love is fine, and love's a

jew- -el while it is new, But when it is old, it grow-eth

cold, and fades a-way like morn-ing dew.

RED RIVER VALLEY

Arranged by Charles Edward Lindsley

think of the Val - ley you're leav- ing? Oh how lone - ly and sad it will be . Do you think of the fond heart you're break- ing And the grief you are caus - ing to me.

SCARBOROUGH FAIR

English Folk Song
Arranged by Fred Bock

*) or Him

SHENANDOAH *Indian Chief*

Sea Chanty
Arranged by Celius Dougherty

O Shen-an-do-ah,— I hear you call-ing, Hi - o! you roll-ing riv-er, O Shen-an-do-ah,— I long to hear you, Hi - o! I'm bound a-way,

o!   I'm bound a - way,   'Cross the wide   Mis-

sou - ri.   Fare - well, my dear - est,_   I'm bound to

leave you;   Hi -   o!   you roll - ing   riv - er,   O

Shen - an - do - ah,___ I'll not de - ceive you,   Hi - o!   I'm bound a -

way,   'Cross the wide   Mis - sou -

ri.

THE TURTLE DOVE

LOW VOICE

Folk song arranged by
Charles Edward Lindsley

roam ten thou - sand miles, my dear, Tho' I roam ten thou - sand

miles.

passionately

So__ fair thou art my bon - ny__ lass, so__ deep in__ love am __

I; But I nev- er will prove false to the bon- ny lass I love, 'Til the

stars fall from the sky, my dear, 'til the stars fall from the

sky. The_ sea will nev-er run dry, my_ dear, nor the

rocks nev-er melt with the sun. But I nev-er will prove false to the

bon- ny lass I love, 'Till__ all these things be done, my dear, 'til__

all these things be done. O__ yon - der doth sit that

lit-tle tur-tle dove, he doth sit on yon-der high tree, A - mak-ing a moan for the

loss of his love, as I will do for thee, my dear, As I will do for

thee.

a tempo

rall.

pp

THE TURTLE DOVE

HIGH VOICE

Folk song arranged by
Charles Edward Lindsley

roam   ten thou - sand miles, my dear, Tho' I roam ten thou - sand

miles.   *passionately*
So—

fair thou art my   bon - ny— lass, So— deep in—love am— I;   But I

nev-er will prove false to the bon-ny lass I love, 'til the stars fall from the

sky, my dear, 'til the stars fall from the sky. The

with determination

sea will nev-er run dry, my dear, Nor the rocks nev-er melt with the

sun.   But I nev-er will prove false to the bon-ny lass I love, 'til —

all   these things be done, my dear, 'til — all these things be

done.   O — yon - der doth sit that   lit-tle tur-tle dove, he doth

p gently

sit on yon-der high tree,   A - mak-ing a moan for the loss of his love, As

I will do for thee, my dear, As I will do for

thee.   *a tempo*   *rall.*

AS LONG AS HE NEEDS ME

(*From* Oliver!)

Lionel Bart

BACK HOME AGAIN

John Denver

THE FIRST TIME EVER I SAW YOUR FACE

Ewan MacColl

The first time ____ ev-er I saw your face, ____

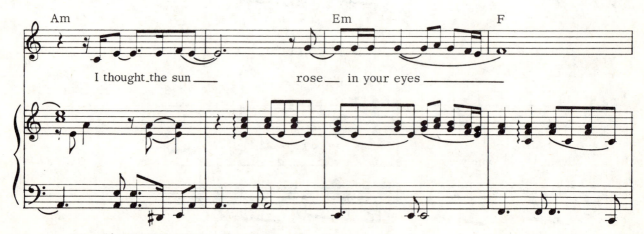

I thought the sun ____ rose ____ in your eyes ____

2. The first time ever I kissed your mouth
    I felt the earth move in my hand,
    Like the trembling heart of a captive bird
    That was there at my command, my love,
    That was there at my command.

3. The first time ever I lay with you
    And felt your heart so close to mine,
    And I knew our joy would fill the earth
    And last till the end of time, my love.
    The first time ever I saw your face,
    Your face, your face, your face.

IF I LOVED YOU

(*From* Carousel)

Oscar Hammerstein II

Richard Rodgers

THE SOUND OF SILENCE

Paul Simon

WE'LL SING IN THE SUNSHINE

Gale Garnett

Moderate

We'll Sing In The Sun - shine,___ We'll laugh ev-'ry day;___

We'll Sing In The Sun - shine___ And I'll be on my way.

Verse

1. I will nev - er love___ you;___ The cost of love's too dear.__
2. sing to you each morn - - ing,___ I'll kiss you ev - 'ry night.
3. dad - dy, he once told___ me, Don't love you an - y man,
4. when our year has end - - ed___ And I have gone a - (wo)way,___

WHO CAN I TURN TO

(*From* The Roar of the Greasepaint, the Smell of the Crowd)

Leslie Bricusse and
Anthony Newley

Slowly with expression

Who can I turn to ___ when no-bod-y needs me? ___ My

heart wants to know and so I must go where des-ti-ny leads me. ___ With

no star to guide me, ___ and no-one be-side me, ___ I'll go on my way, and

From the musical production *The Roar of the
Greasepaint, the Smell of the Crowd*. Words and music
by Leslie Bricusse and Anthony Newley. © Copyright
1964 Concord Music Ltd., London, England. TRO–
Musical Comedy Productions, Inc., New York, controls
all publication rights for the U.S.A. and Canada. Used
by permission.

YESTERDAY

John Lennon and Paul McCartney

YOU'LL NEVER WALK ALONE
(From Carousel)

Oscar Hammerstein II

Richard Rodgers

When you walk through a storm, hold your head up high And don't be a-fraid of the dark, At the end of the storm is a

N-N-N-NOW, MY DEAR
(From The Bartered Bride)

Karel Sabina
English by Marian Farquhar

Bedřich Smetana (1824–1884)

f... for you to wed!

Br... br... brace up, brace up. And b...

be a man! Wha... what oth-ers do, You sure-ly

can." ____ Br... br... brace up, brace up, a...

OH! MIO BABBINO CARO

Oh! My Beloved Daddy
(*From* Gianni Schicchi)

Giovacchino Forzano
English by Anne and
Herbert Grossman

Giacomo Puccini (1858–1924)

Andantino ingenuo ♪ = 120

Oh! mio bab-bi - no ca - - ro, mi pia-ce, e bel - lo,
Oh! my be - lov - ed dad - - dy, won't you be kind and

bel - lo; vo'an-da - re in Por - ta Ros - sa a com-pe-rar l'a -
help us? You know I love Ri - nuc - cio, I can not live with -

nel - lo! Si, si, ci voglio an - da - - re! e se l'a-mas - si in -
out him! Oh please, do not re - fuse me. He is my life, my

Used by permission of Associated Music Publishers,
Inc., U.S. agents for G. Ricordi, Milan.

VA! LAISSE COULER MES LARMES

No, Let All My Tears Continue

(*From* Werther)

English version by
Lorraine Noel Finley

Jules Massenet
(1842–1912)

Va!_ lais-se cou-ler mes lar-mes;
No,_ let all my tears con-tin - ue,

El-les font du bien, ma ché-ri - e!
They do so much good, O my dear-est!

Les lar-mes qu'on ne pleu-re pas, Dans notre â - me re-tom-bent tou - tes, Et de leurs
For tears un-shed will sure-ly fall, In the soul they will sink, re-treat - ing, Per-sist-ent

WHEN THE AIR SINGS OF SUMMER

(*From* The Old Maid and the Thief)

Gian-Carlo Menotti (1911–   )

Andante calmo, ma senza trascinare

When the air sings of sum-mer, I must wan-der a-gain.

Sweet landlord is the sky, rich house is the plain, and to live is to wan-der

through the sun and the rain. When the air sings of sum-mer I must wan-der a-gain.

First you wan-der in youth and joy then you'll wan-der to still the fears

in an old heart. First you wan - der to find your love,

then you'll wan - der to hide your tears, for a wand'-rer must de-part.

When a man owns a house he is a bird in a cage whose cap-ti-vi-ty pain

PHÄNOMEN

The Rainbow

LOW VOICE

Goethe
English by Charles Edward Lindsley

Johannes Brahms (1833–1897)
Edited by Charles Edward Lindsley

far - big be-schat - tet.
tint - ing the sky - line.

far - big be-schat - tet.
tint - ing the sky - line.

Im Ne - bel glei - chen Kreis seh ich ge - zo - gen,
Though fog will dim its hues to fad - ed___ grey - white,

Im Ne - bel glei - chen Kreis
Though fog will dim its hues

Zwar ist der Bo - - gen weiss, doch___
No col - ors will___ it lose,___ still

seh ich___ge - zo - gen, Zwar ist der Bo - gen weiss,___ doch___
to fad - ed___ grey-white, No col - ors will___ it lose,___ still

dich nicht be-trü - - ben, sind gleich die Haa - re weiss,
don't let age grieve you, All is not said and done;

dich_____ nicht be-trü - -ben: sind gleich die Haa - re weiss,
don't_____ let age grieve you, All is not said and done;

doch wirst du lie - ben, doch wirst, doch wirst_____ du
love will not leave you. Love will, love will_____ not

doch wirst du lie - ben, doch wirst, doch wirst_____ du_____
love will not leave you. Love will, love will_____ not

lie - ben.
leave you.

lie - ben.
leave you.

PHÄNOMEN

The Rainbow

HIGH VOICE

Goethe
English by Charles Edward Lindsley

Johannes Brahms (1833–1897)
Edited by Charles Edward Lindsley

far - -big be-schat -tet.
tint . ing the sky -line.

far - - -big be-schat -tet.
tint - ing the sky - line.

Im Ne - bel glei - chen Kreis seh ich ge - zo - gen,
Though fog will dim its hues to fad -ed grey -white,

Im Ne - bel glei - chen Kreis
Though fog will dim its hues

zwar ist der Bo - - gen weiss,___
No col - ors will_____ it lose,___

seh ich ge - zo - gen, zwar ist der Bo - - gen
to fad -ed_ grey - white, no col - ors will_____ it

doch___ Him-mels-bo——gen,   zwar ist der
Still   it is hea-   ven's light,   no col-ors

weiss, doch___ Him-mels-bo-gen,   zwar ist der Bo-gen, der
lose, Still   it is heav'n's light,   no col-ors will it lose,

Bo——gen weiss,___ doch___ Him-mels-bo-gen, doch___
will___ it   lose;___ still___ it   is heav'n's light, still___

Bo——gen weiss,___ doch___ Him-mels-bo-gen, doch___
will___ it   lose;___ still___ it is heav'n's light; still___

poco f

___ Him-mels-bo——gen.   So sollst du, munt-rer Greis,
it   is heav'n's light.   Take heart then, white- haired one,

___ Him-mels-bo——gen.   So sollst du, munt-rer Greis,
it   is heav'n's light.   Take heart then, white- haired one,

p dolce

SELMA UND SELMAR

Selma and Selmar

LOW VOICE

Friedrich Gottlieb Klopstock
English by Charles Edward Lindsley

Franz Schubert (1797–1828)
Edited by Charles Edward Lindsley

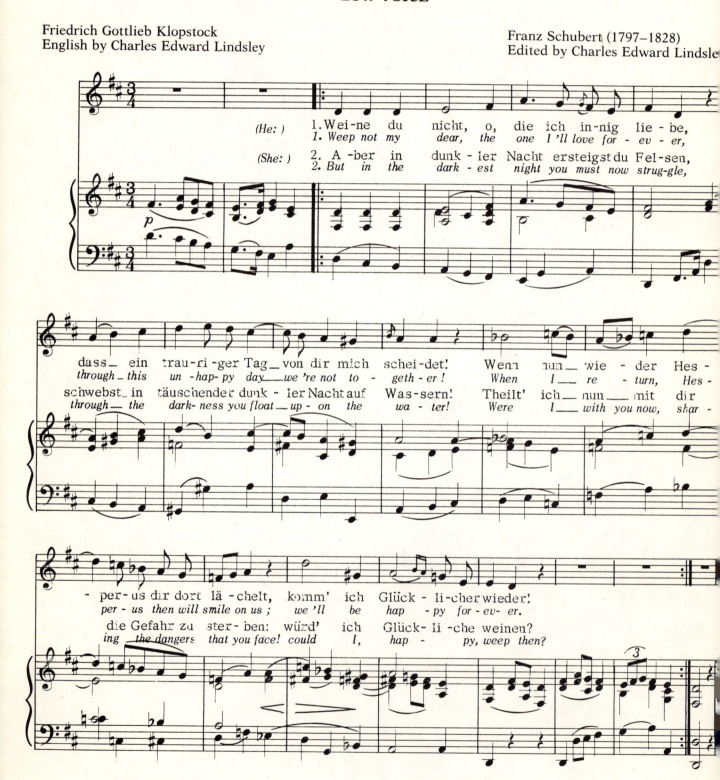

SELMA UND SELMAR

Selma and Selmar

HIGH VOICE

Friedrich Gottlieb Klopstock
English by Charles Edward Lindsley

Franz Schubert (1797–1828)
Edited by Charles Edward Lindsley

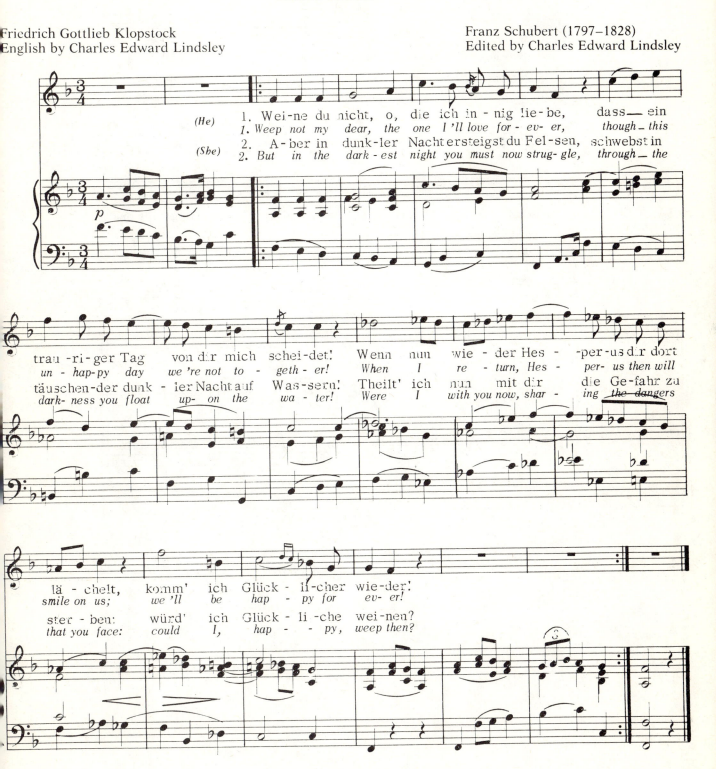

(He)
1. Wei-ne du nicht, o, die ich in-nig lie-be, dass ein
1. Weep not my dear, the one I'll love for-ev-er, though this

(She)
2. A-ber in dunk-ler Nacht ersteigst du Fel-sen, schwebst in
2. But in the dark-est night you must now strug-gle, through the

trau-ri-ger Tag von dir mich schei-det! Wenn nun wie-der Hes-per-us dir dort
un-hap-py day we're not to-geth-er! When I re-turn, Hes-per-us then will
täuschen-der dunk-ler Nacht auf Was-sern! Theilt' ich nun mit dir die Ge-fahr zu
dark-ness you float up-on the wa-ter! Were I with you now, shar-ing the dangers

lä-chelt, komm' ich Glück-li-cher wie-der!
smile on us; we'll be hap-py for ev-er!
ster-ben: würd' ich Glück-li-che wei-nen?
that you face: could I, hap-py, weep then?

AMERICA

Henry Carey

AMERICA THE BEAUTIFUL

Katherine Lee Bates

Samuel A. Ward

BIBLIOGRAPHY

Adler, Kurt. *The Art of Accompanying and Coaching.* Minneapolis: University of Minnesota Press, 1965.

Alderson, Richard. *Complete Handbook of Voice Training.* West Nyack, N.Y.: Parker Publishing Co., 1979.

Appleman, R. *The Science of Vocal Pedagogy.* Bloomington: Indiana University Press, 1967.

Barlow, W. *The Alexander Technique.* New York: Alfred A. Knopf, 1973.

Bartholomew, Wilmer T. *Acoustics of Music.* Englewood Cliffs, N.J.: Prentice-Hall, 1942.

Boone, Daniel. "Vocal Hygiene: The Optimal Use of the Larynx." *Journal of Research in Singing,* December 1980, pp. 35–43.

Bunch, Maribeth. *Dynamics of the Singing Voice.* Vienna and New York: Springer-Verlag, 1982.

Burgin, John Carroll. *Teaching Singing.* Metuchen, N.J.: Scarecrow Press, 1973.

Caruso, Enrico, and Luisa Tetrazzini. *The Art of Singing.* 1909; reprint, New York: Dover Publications, 1975.

Christy, Van A. *Expressive Singing.* 3d ed., 2 vols. Dubuque, Iowa: Wm. C. Brown, 1967.

————. *Foundations in Singing.* 4th ed. Dubuque, Iowa: Wm. C. Brown, 1979.

Creager, Joan G. *Human Anatomy and Physiology.* Belmont, Calif.: Wadsworth, 1983.

Culver, Charles A. *Musical Acoustics.* New York: McGraw-Hill, 1956.

Dickson, David R. *Human Vocal Anatomy.* Springfield, Ill.: Charles C Thomas, 1970.

Diehl, Charles F. *Introduction to the Anatomy and Physiology of the Speech Mechanisms.* Springfield, Ill: Charles C Thomas, 1968.

Fields, Victor A. *Training the Singing Voice.* New York: Kings Crown Press, 1947.

Fillebrown, Thomas. *Resonance in Singing and Speaking.* New York: Oliver Ditson Co., 1911.

Fuchs, Viktor. *The Art of Singing and Voice Technique.* New York: London House and Maxwell, 1964.

Garcia, Manuel. *Hints on Singing.* London: Ascherberg, Hopwood, and Crew, 1894.

Gardner, Weston D. *Structure of the Human Body.* Philadelphia: W. B. Saunders, 1967.

Godt, Irving. "The Latest Renaissance Instrument: The Voice." *Divisions: A Journal for the Art and Practice of Early Musick* 1, no. 4 (1980): pp. 14–22.

Gray, Henry. *Anatomy, Descriptive and Surgical.* American ed. 1901; reprint, New York: Crown Publishers, 1977.

Hammar, Russel A. *Singing, an Extension of Speech.* Metuchen, N.J.: Scarecrow Press, 1978.

Henderson, Laura Browning. *How to Train Singers.* West Nyack, N.Y.: Parker Publishing Co., 1979.

Herbert-Caesari, E. *The Science and Sensations of Vocal Tone.* 2d rev. ed. Boston: Crescendo Publishing Co., 1968.

Hewitt, Graham. *How to Sing.* New York: Taplinger Publishing Co., 1978.

Husler, Frederick, and Yvonne Rodd-Marling. *Singing: The Physical Nature of the Vocal Organ.* London: Faber and Faber, 1965.

Jacobi, Henry N. *Building Your Best Voice.* Englewood Cliffs, N.J.: Prentice-Hall, 1982.

Kagen, Sergius. *On Studying Singing.* New York: Rinehart and Co., 1950.

Klein, Joseph J. *Singing Technique: How to Avoid Vocal Trouble*. Princeton, N.J.: D. Van Nostrand Co., 1967.

Kosarin, Oscar. *The Singing Actor*. Englewood Cliffs, N.J.: Prentice-Hall, 1983.

Large, John, and Robert Patton. "The Effect of Weight Training and Aerobic Exercise on Singers." *Journal of Research in Singing*, June 1981, pp. 23–31.

Lehmann, Lilli. *How to Sing*. (*Meine Gesangskunst*, translated by Richard Aldrich.) New York: Macmillan, 1924.

Lessac, Arthur. *The Use and Training of the Human Voice*. 2d ed. New York: DBS Publications, 1967.

Leyerle, William D. *Vocal Development through Organic Imagery*. New York: Privately published, 1977.

Linklater, Kristin. *Freeing the Natural Voice*. New York: Drama Book Specialists, 1925.

Litante, Judith. *A Natural Approach to Singing*. Dubuque, Iowa: Wm. C. Brown, 1959.

Manen, Lucie. *The Art of Singing*. Bryn Mawr, Pa.: Theodore Presser Co., 1976.

Marafioti, P. Mario. *Caruso's Method of Voice Production*. 1922; reprint, New York: Dover Publications, 1981.

Mayer, Lyle V. *Fundamentals of Voice and Diction*. Dubuque, Iowa: Wm. C. Brown, 1978.

Miller, Kenneth E. *Principles of Singing*. Englewood Cliffs, N.J.: Prentice-Hall, 1983.

Miller, Richard. *English, French, German and Italian Technique of Singing*. Metuchen, N.J.: Scarecrow Press, 1977.

Monahan, Brent Jeffrey. *The Art of Singing*. Metuchen, N.J., and London: Scarecrow Press, 1978.

Muckey, Floyd S. *The Natural Method of Voice Production*. New York: Charles Scribner's, 1915.

Nicholas, Louis. "The Voice Class." In *The Choral Directors Guide*, ed. Kenneth L. Neidig and John W. Jennings. West Nyack, N.Y.: Parker Publishing Co., 1967.

Peterson, Paul W. *Natural Singing and Expressive Conducting*. Winston-Salem, N.C.: John F. Blair, Publisher, 1955.

Pucci, Sharon A. *How to Save Your Voice*. San Francisco: Bluetick Publishing, 1983.

Punt, N. A. *The Singer's and Actor's Throat*. 3d ed. London: Heinemann Medical Books, 1979.

Reid, Cornelius L. *The Free Voice*. New York: Coleman-Ross Co., 1965.

Russell, Florence. *The Subject Is Singing*. Los Alamitos, Calif.: Hwong Publishing Co., 1979.

Sable, Barbara Kinsey. *The Vocal Sound*. Englewood Cliffs, N.J.: Prentice-Hall, 1982.

Saunders, William H. *The Larynx*. Summit, N.J.: CIBA Pharmaceutical Co., 1964.

Schiøtz, Aksel. *The Singer and His Art*. New York: Harper & Row, 1970.

Shipp, T., R. Leanderson, and J. Sundberg. "Some Acoustic Characteristics of Vocal Vibrato." *Journal of Research in Singing*, December 1980, pp. 18–25.

"The Singing Stops, the Song Continues." *Music Insider*, charter issue, 1981, p. 2.

Smolover, Raymond. *The Vocal Essence*. Scarsdale, N.Y.: Covenant Publications, 1971.

Stanley, Douglas. *The Science of Voice*. New York: Carl Fischer, Inc., 1929.

———. *Your Voice*. New York: Pitman Publishing Corp., 1945.

Stanton, Royal. *Steps to Singing*. 3d ed. Belmont, Calif.: Wadsworth, 1983.

Sundberg, Johan. "The Acoustics of the Singing Voice." *Scientific American*, March

1977, pp. 82–91. Reprinted in *Readings from Scientific American: The Physics of Music*, pp. 16–23. San Francisco: W. H. Freeman, 1978.

Trusler, Ivan, and Walter Ehret. *Functional Lessons in Singing.* Englewood Cliffs, N.J.: Prentice-Hall, 1960.

Vennard, William. *Developing Voices.* New York: Carl Fischer, Inc., 1973.

———. *Singing. The Mechanism and the Technique.* Rev. ed. New York: Carl Fischer, Inc., 1967.

Wedin, Sven. "EMG Investigation of Abdominal Musculature during Phonation." Paper for the 16th International Congress of Logopedics and Phoniatrics, Boden, Sweden, 1974.

Wedin, Sven, Rolf Leanderson, and Lodge Wedin. "Evaluation of Voice Training: Spectral Analysis Compared with Listeners' Judgments." Paper for the 17th International Congress of Logopedics and Phoniatrics, Boden, Sweden, 1977.

White, Ernest G. *Science and Singing.* 6th ed. Boston: Crescendo Publishing Co., 1950.

Winsel, Regnier. *The Anatomy of Voice.* New York: Exposition Press, 1978.

Zimmerman, Rea. *Sing Out Like Never Before.* Tucson: Up with People, 1980.

Tracy

Voices female

classical

chest   middle   head

passagio (bridge)

male   chest   head

passagio   falsetto

Long phrases —

take it faster or leave out first few words, continue

— Sun 3PM — Recital — paper francor research

Brahms
Charles Ives
Samuel Barber

critique Due March 30